On some positions cowardice asks the question, is it safe? Expediency asks the question, is it politic? Vanity asks the question, is it popular? But conscience asks the question, is it right? And there comes a time when one must take a position that is neither safe, nor politic, nor popular but he must take it because conscience tells him it is right.

-Rev. Dr. Martin Luther King, Jr.

As a father has compassion on his children,
so the Lord has compassion on those who fear him;
for he knows how we are formed,
he remembers that we are dust.

-Psalm 103: 13-14

Why Be Good? And Other Questions Concerning Moral Philosophy

Max Malikow

Why Be Good? And Other Questions Concerning Moral Philosophy

ISBN 9781733454087

To Alex Pregnar: My favorite kvetcher and a man of integrity.

To Artie and Cathy Bender: Who do good because they know no other way.

To L.P.: To whom it never occurs to ask, "Why be good?" She just is.

Acknowledgment

There is no accurate answer to the question, "When does a book begin?" The convergence of experiences and other influences that initiate and sustain a writing project are indiscernible. Any attempt to acknowledge those who deserve recognition would result in unintentionally omitting others who merit the same. I am left to acknowledge my debt of gratitude to the innumerable individuals who have shaped my thinking on moral philosophy.

Preface

Recently, as I wandered through a used bookstore, a humbling thought occurred to me. Amidst thousands of books on shelves and tables and stacked in piles on the floor it dawned on me that this is the fate of all books, even bestsellers. Although I didn't encounter any of my books there I knew they could be found in other used bookstores, Salvation Army thrift shops, attics or basements.

Given that "there is nothing new under the sun" (Ecclesiastes 1:9) and "all we do crumbles to the ground" ("Dust in the Wind") why do I write? First, like George Orwell, but with far less talent, I write because I must and not to write would go against my nature. Second, like Wallace Stegner, I write to make sense of it all. Third, I write to organize my thoughts which makes me a better teacher. There might be other reasons why I write but these three are sufficient to keep me writing even in the wake of my recent bookstore experience.

Max Malikow
Syracuse, NY
January 24, 2021

Table of Contents

Introduction

It's difficult, if not impossible, to disagree with William James' assertion that there are three unknowables that lead to a fourth. He taught it is impossible to know if God exists, if free will is a reality, and if there is an afterlife. These three unknowables force a fourth upon us: it is impossible to know if there is such a thing as moral obligation.

James reasoned if God does not exist there is no moral authority over all human beings and cultures. As some have said, "If God does not exist then all things are possible." (This is often attributed to Fyodor Dostoevsky who communicates this idea in *The Brothers Karamazov*.) James further reasoned if free will does not exist then we do not engage in authentic moral decision-making and, therefore, cannot be responsible for our behavior. Finally, he added, if there is no afterlife there is no punishment for misdeeds that went unpunished before death.

Any argument forwarded by William James is not to be taken lightly. Note that his proposition about moral obligation is stated conditionally – if there is no God, free will or afterlife then there are no moral obligations. This book arises from the possibility – not the certainty – that moral obligations do exist. Alternatively stated, if God, free will, and an afterlife exist then a discussion of moral decision-making and responsibility for moral conduct is a worthy pursuit. This book carries on this discussion.

There are those who maintain academic courses on moral philosophy have no influence on the students who take them. A *Wall Street Journal* editorial, titled, "Does an 'A' in Ethics Have Any Value?" argues it's impossible to measure the influence of ethics courses on their students (Korn, 2013). On the other side of this issue is Michael Schaub, who believes, "if you cannot (teach ethics) it is virtually the only realm of education that is held to be unteachable" (2012). (Schaub, an ethics professor, admits to not being objective about the value of his courses.) Agreeing with Schaub are authorities as diverse as Socrates, a philosopher dating back 2500 years, and contemporary psychologists Thomas Lickona, Philip Zimbardo, and William Kilpatrick as well as psychiatrist Robert Coles.

Schaub also makes the interesting observation that critics of academic ethics courses tend to believe "that you cannot teach ethics 'up' (but) you can teach ethics 'down,' as evidenced by extensive cheating reported in colleges" (2012). His point is, if "badness" can be taught then why can't "goodness" also be taught? In psychologist James Rest's overview of contemporary research in the field of moral development, he found formal education in ethics enhances moral reasoning capability and influences moral judgment (Velasquez, Andre, Shanks, and Meyer, 1987). I agree with those who believe there are sufficient data to justify teaching courses and writing books on morality. (Why else would I do both?) This book invites you to a discussion of the nature and value of moral philosophy.

I also believe academic books should be as "user-friendly" as possible. Hence, this book is written in the first person point-of-view and employs contractions, which are characteristic of conversations rather than scholarly treatises.*

*Unless otherwise indicated, biblical quotations are from the New International Version translation of the The Holy Bible.

I. What Is Moral Philosophy?

*About morality I only know right is what you feel good after
and wrong is what you feel bad after*

- Ernest Hemingway

In 1939 Dr. Max Schur had a decision to make. One of his patients, an 83 year-old man suffering with inoperable oral cancer, requested a lethal dose of morphine. The patient was Sigmund Freud. The question of euthanizing him met the criteria for a moral issue:

1. It involved the "rightness" or "wrongness" of an action.
2. It involved a widely accepted ethical principle.
3. It involved at least one person other than the decision-maker.
4. It involved the assumption of responsibility.

Dr. Schur decided the morally right action in this case was to end his patient's suffering by ending his patient's life. This decision violated the Hippocratic Oath's principle of "do no harm" as well as the biblical sixth commandment, "Thou shalt not kill." In addition, Schur's decision went beyond himself, extending to Freud and the family that lost its patriarch. Finally, although he acted on Freud's request, Schur was responsible for Freud dying when he did, around midnight on September 23, 1939.

Ethics is the subcategory of philosophy that addresses the question, "How are morally right actions distinguished from morally wrong actions?" (Technically, although "ethics" and "morals" are not synonymous they are used interchangeably in common parlance as well as in this book.) Few of us will ever be confronted with a decision of the magnitude of Dr. Scur's. Nevertheless, the principles that guided him in his decision-making are the same for all moral deliberation. However quotidian the situation, it is a moral issue if it involves the four criteria listed above. We don't have to decide whether to drop atomic bombs on Hiroshima and Nagasaki, as did President Harry Truman, or sentence a convicted murderer to execution, as do some judges, to be engaged in moral decision-making. Psychologist William Kirk Kilpatrick makes this point in *Why Johnny Can't Tell Right from Wrong*. He maintains most moral decisions entail ordinary situations:

> Most of our "moral decisions" have to do with temptations to do things we know we shouldn't do or temptations to avoid doing the things we know we should do. A temptation to steal money from her mother's purse is a more common problem for the average girl than deciding whether or not to turn in a friend who is shoplifting (1992, p. 85).

Similarly, Kilpatrick disdains the use of dilemmas in moral discussions. It has been said a dilemma is a predicament in which no matter what you choose to do you will be wrong. A well-known dilemma confronted survivors of the Titanic who had to decide who would remain in an overcrowded lifeboat and who would be set adrift in the frigid North Atlantic and certain death. Another is the dilemma of the plane crash survivors who had to decide if they would resort to cannibalism or die from starvation. Although these are actual situations Kilpatrick maintains they are too rare to provide guidance for everyday moral decision-making:

> Like a roller-coaster ride, the dilemma approach can leave its passengers a bit breathless. That is one of its attractions. But like a roller-coaster ride, it may leave them all a bit disoriented – or more than a bit. The question to ask about this admittedly stimulating approach is this: Do we want to concentrate on quandaries or on everyday morality? (p. 84).

How is "morally good" determined?

In the Gospel According to Luke a rich man approaches Jesus with a question. Before answering, Jesus asks him to define his use of the term "good."

> A certain ruler asked him, "Good teacher, what must I do to inherit eternal life?" "Why do you call me good?" Jesus answered. "No one is good – except God alone" (8:18-19).

Jesus was not being persnickety, like Socrates he understood the importance of defining terms. Shakespeare alluded to this when he wrote of giving to "airy abstraction" a "local habitation and a name" (*A Midsummer Night's Dream,* Act IV, scene 1). When "morally good" lingers as an airy abstraction it renders conversations about morality vague and meaningless.

One understanding of "morally good" is virtuous. A virtue is a commendable trait or quality, a behavior that conforms to a standard of right conduct. The classical virtues are courage, self-control, fairness, and wisdom. (Collectively these are known as the cardinal virtues and alternatively referred to as fortitude, temperance, justice, and prudence respectively.) An impressive research project by psychologists Martin Seligman and Chris Peterson affirmed these four virtues and added to them "love for humanity" and "spirituality and transcendence" (2004). In my own writing I have added three other virtues: integrity, perseverance, and resilience (2017).

In his eloquent "Letter from Birmingham Jail" the Rev. Dr. Martin Luther King, Jr. addresses morality when making a distinction between just and unjust laws:

> One may well ask, "How can you advocate breaking some laws and obeying others?" The answer is found in the fact that there are two types of laws: there are just and unjust laws. I would agree with St. Augustine that "An unjust law is no law at all." Now what is the difference between the two? How does one determine

when a law is just or unjust? A just law is a man-made code that squares with the moral law or the law of God. An unjust law is a code that is out of harmony with the moral law. To put it in the terms of Saint Thomas Aquinas, an unjust law is a human law that is not rooted in eternal and natural law. Any law that uplifts human personality is just. Any law that degrades human personality is unjust (1997, p. 214).

The epigraph to this chapter is from Ernest Hemingway's *Death in the Afternoon*. ("About morality I only know right is what you feel good after and wrong is what you feel bad after" [1932, p. 2]). While this observation should not be dismissed it does not serve well as a moral guideline. A psychopath can feel good after egregious behavior and an overly scrupulous person can feel bad in spite of praiseworthy conduct. Moreover, we don't have to be psychopathic to elude feeling bad after behaving abominably. Even children demonstrate the capacity to rationalize and justify their misbehavior. The science fiction writer Robert Heinlein went as far as characterizing the ability to make misconduct acceptable to the conscience a defining feature of human beings: "Man is not a rational animal, he is a rationalizing animal" (2005, p. 542). Another writer of note, George Orwell, addresses the convenience of rationalizing when sharing a thought he had when writing during a World War II air raid:

As I write, highly civilized human beings are flying overhead, trying to kill me. They do not feel any enmity against me as an individual, nor I against them. They are "only doing their duty," as the saying goes. Most of them, I have no doubt, are kind-hearted, law abiding men who would never dream of committing murder in private life. On the other hand, if one of them succeeds in blowing me to pieces with a well-placed bomb, he will never sleep any the worse for it. He is serving his country, which has the power to absolve him from evil (1946, p. 11).

On a more cynical note Orwell also writes, "Political language is designed to make lies sound truthful and murder respectable and to give an appearance of solidity to pure wind" (1946, front cover).

A behavior is morally good only if it conforms to a preexisting standard. It would be absurd to construct a standard following a behavior as shown in the "Parable of Shlomo."

Once upon a time there was a man sent by his king to recruit archers for the royal army. The man searched far and wide but could not find even one man sufficiently skilled with a bow-and-arrow to serve the king. Close to giving up, the man came upon a village where he saw targets painted on the sides of several buildings, trees, and hillsides. Moreover, he was encouraged because each of the targets had an arrow in the target's dead center, "bull's eye" location. Excitedly, he asked the first villager he encountered, "Who is the master archer who lives among you? He is needed for the king's army." The villager responded, "We have no such man in this village!" Perplexed, the king's emissary asked, "But what about all those targets with arrows in the dead center?" Laughing, the villager replied, "Oh, those! That's the work of Shlomo, our village idiot. He goes around shooting arrows in every direction and then paints a target around the arrows."

Nevertheless, even a preexisting standard is an unreliable moral compass if it is morally questionable or unquestionably immoral. The Holocaust conformed to the legal standard in Nazi era Germany but few would argue this made the Holocaust right. Dr. King recognized this and cautioned:

We can never forget that everything Hitler did in Germany was "legal" and everything the Hungarian freedom fighters did in Hungary was "illegal." It was "illegal" to aid and comfort a Jew in Hitler's Germany. But I am sure if I lived in Germany during that time I would have aided and comforted my Jewish brothers even though it was illegal (1997, p. 216).

Another example of a dubious standard is the "three-fifths compromise" established by the United States Constitutional Convention. It determined slaves would be counted in the population at the ratio of three for every five. This standard, although legal in 1787, would be indefensible if proposed today.

Moral principles derived from religious teaching usually provide a virtuous code of conduct. Followers of Christianity and Judaism strive to abide by the Ten Commandments, one of which forbids adultery. Christianity reinforces this in the New Testament's "Letter to the Corinthians" where it is written that adulterers "will not inherit the kingdom of God" (1 Corinthians 6:9). Of course, this raises the question of what constitutes adultery. In Christianity the biblical definition extends beyond mere sexual intimacy with someone other than one's spouse. A divorced woman is an adulteress if she remarries while her former husband is still alive:

> by law a married woman is bound to her husband as long as he is alive, but if her husband dies, she is released from the law of marriage. So then, if she marries another man while her husband is still alive she is called an adulteress. But if her husband dies, she is released from that law and is not an adulteress, even though she marries another man (Romans 7:2-3).

The same is true for a divorced man who remarries. In his teaching on divorce Jesus said, "I tell you that anyone who divorces his wife, except for marital unfaithfulness, and marries another woman, commits adultery" (Matthew 19:9). It must be added that the remedy for this and every other sin is found in John's epistle: "If we confess our sins, he (God) is faithful and just and will forgive us our sins and purify us from all unrighteousness" (1 John 1:9). While this promise of forgiveness is encouraging it does not provide instruction for the remarried who have confessed their adultery. Are they supposed to leave their current marriage or remain in it but celibate?

Dr. Otto Gross is a striking example of someone unrestrained by religious teaching. A contemporary of Freud and Carl Jung, he showed considerable promise as a psychoanalyst before devoting himself to an anarchistic movement. Although married, he considered sexual involvement with his female patients as well as any other woman who caught his fancy a healthy expression of a fundamental drive. In the acclaimed movie, *A Dangerous Method*, he is portrayed by Vincent Cassel and in a conversation with Jung refers to monogamy as a "depressing concept" and rationalizes his philandering with, "If there's one thing I've learned in my short life it is this: never repress anything" (2011). Still, even someone who views infidelity as a sin might have difficulty accepting that homosexuals, thieves, drunkards, slanderers, and the verbally abusive face eternal condemnation. They are listed with adulterers as those who "will not inherit the kingdom of God" (1 Corinthians 6:9,10).

Finally, it is reasonable to ask if religious standards are binding upon those who do not adhere to any religion? This question was addressed at the post-World War II Nuremberg Trials, where prominent military and political members of the Nazi party were charged with crimes against humanity. A common misunderstanding is the Nazi war criminals who perpetrated the Holocaust defended themselves at Nuremberg by claiming they were merely following orders. Actually, the defense they offered was they did nothing wrong. They argued the highest authority in Germany was the government and since the Holocaust was a government program the mass killing of Jews was legal where it occurred. They further argued the Nuremberg court had no jurisdiction over them because the laws of other nations did not apply to them. (Noteworthy is Holocaust deniers seem unaware that the men who perpetrated the Holocaust admitted at trial the Holocaust occurred.) An implication of their defense is the sixth commandment, "Thou shalt not kill," did not apply to them (Exodus 20: 13).

If there are no universal principles for determining morality then moral relativism provides the moral compass. Briefly stated, it is the belief that right and wrong are culturally determined because absolute moral principles do not exist. Chapter VII, where the question, "Can people be good without God?" is addressed, includes an analysis of moral relativism.

II. Why Be Good?

It is impossible to live the pleasant life without living sensibly, nobly and justly, and it is impossible to live sensibly, nobly and justly without living pleasantly.

- Epicurus

Asking the question, "Why be good?" is not like asking, "Why brush my teeth?" or "Why pay my credit card bill?" The consequences of not brushing or not paying a credit card bill are obvious. The advantage of behaving morally is also obvious when recognition or reward will follow. Equally obvious is the disadvantage of behaving immorally when it will result in punishment. But why behave morally when it will not be rewarded or, even worse, when it will result in punishment? Or why not engage in misconduct when there is no possibility of punishment and it will provide a benefit?

One reason for moral uprightness is the satisfaction of conscience. Rationalizing doesn't always silence the moral voice. Nathaniel Hawthorne's *The Scarlet Letter* describes the wretched state of Arthur Dimmesdale, a Puritan minister who violated his conscience by engaging in an extramarital affair and fathering an illegitimate child. Although his sin goes undiscovered and he retains his standing as the community's spiritual leader his conscience is unrelenting:

It is the unspeakable misery of a life so false as his, that it steals the pith and substance out of whatever realities there are around us, and which were meant by Heaven to be the spirit's joy and nutriment. To the untrue man, the whole universe is false – it is impalpable – it shrinks to nothing within his grasp. And insofar as he shows himself in a false light, becomes a shadow, or, indeed, ceases to exist (1978, p. 107).

When Epicurus spoke of the pleasant life he did not mean a life of enjoyment and ease. Many a person has lived a painful, depressed life in spite of having lived "sensibly, nobly and justly" (2015). No one lived a more virtuous life than Jesus Christ, yet he was "a man of sorrows, and familiar with suffering" (Isaiah 53:3). Aristotle and Epicurus taught a pleasant life requires living in a manner that is consistent with an internalized moral code. The *Nicomachean Ethics* includes this instruction from Aristotle: "He is happy who lives in accordance with complete virtue not for some chance period but throughout a complete life" (2009, 1101a10).

Conscience and conduct are addressed in Plato's *The Republic* in a debate between Glaucon, Plato's brother, and Socrates concerning the mythical Ring of Gyges, a ring that grants invisibility to anyone wearing it. Glaucon argues if there were two such rings and a just man wore one and an unjust man wore the other there would be no difference in their behavior. Guaranteed anonymity and the impossibility of punishment, both men would steal from the marketplace, spy on women, and release prisoners from confinement. Socrates counters there is a difference between reputation and integrity. Reputation is what other people think of us; integrity is what we know about ourselves. The Ring of Gyges provides a safeguard against a bad reputation but it cannot protect us from knowing our own dishonorable conduct.

Robert Sapolsky, a professor of biology and neurology at Stanford University, has described the human brain's frontal cortex as "the region of the brain (that) makes us do the hard thing when the right thing is the hard thing to do" (Harris, 2020, p. 262). If Sapolsky is right then psychiatrist and Holocaust survivor Viktor Frankl's frontal cortex was involved in his decision to remain in Nazi controlled Vienna in 1940. Frankl let his immigration visa to the United States expire because leaving Austria would have meant abandoning his elderly parents. His good deed did not go unpunished. He spent three years in the Auschwitz and Dachau work camps. This was not the first time Frankl put himself in harm's way. When he was the Director of the Neurology Department of the Rothschild Hospital in Vienna he gave false diagnoses to Jewish mentally ill patients to prevent them from being euthanized as part of a government policy.

Dietrich Bonhoeffer, a Lutheran pastor and theologian, also was penalized for doing the right thing. A staunch and vocal Nazi dissident, he left the safety of the United States to return to Germany where he was arrested by the Gestapo in

1943 and hanged in 1945. He shared the rationale for his fatal decision with Reinhold Niebuhr, an American theologian:

> I have come to the conclusion that I made a mistake in coming to America. I must live through this difficult period in our national history with the people of Germany. I will have no right to participate in the reconstruction of Christian life in Germany after the war if I do not share the trials of this time with my people. Christians in Germany will have to face the terrible alternative of either willing the defeat of their nation in order that Christian civilization may survive or willing the victory of their nation and thereby destroying civilization. I know which of these alternatives I must choose but I cannot make that choice from security (Bethge, 2000, p. 655).

The tombstone inscription of the 18th century philosopher Immanuel Kant reads: "Two things fill my mind with ever increasing awe, the starry heavens above me and the moral law within me" (1785). Kant marveled that his moral conduct was of such interest to the Creator of the universe that God provided him with a conscience. The Reverend Dr. Martin Luther King, Jr. also spoke of conscience as a moral compass. In a speech given 11 months before his death he spoke of conduct and conscience in a manner that could be considered definitive:

On some positions cowardice asks the question, is it safe? Expediency asks the question, is it politic? Vanity asks the question, is it popular? But conscience asks the question, is it right? And there comes a time when one must take a position that is neither safe, nor politic, nor popular but he must take it because conscience tells him it is right (1967).

A second reason to "be good" is the fear of damnation. Of course, this motivation applies only to those who believe in God, an afterlife, and a place of eternal torment. One of Christianity's most celebrated sermons is Jonathan Edwards' "Sinners in the Hands of an Angry God." Preached in 1741, its graphic portrayal of hell was influential in the Great Awakening, an evangelical revival that swept through Colonial America in the 1730's and 1740's. Edwards forcefully presented God as graciously delaying the damnation of the unrepentant and unconverted:

So that it is not because God is unmindful of their wickedness, and does not resent it, that he does not let loose his hand and cut them off. God is not altogether such an one as themselves, though they may imagine him to be so. The wrath of God burns against them, their damnation does not slumber; the pit is prepared, the fire is made ready, the furnace is now hot, ready to receive them; the flames do now rage and glow. The glittering sword is whet, and held over them, and the pit hath opened its mouth under them (1992, pp. 7-8).

This fear is expressed in song in the musical *Les Miserables*. The protagonist, Jean Valjean, is faced with the dilemma of allowing an innocent man to go to prison in his place or speaking up and going to prison himself. In this quandary he sings, "If I speak, I am condemned; if I stay silent, I am damned" (1980). Realizing eternal damnation is worse than imprisonment, he presents himself before the magistrate on behalf of the innocent man and prepares himself to go to prison.

A third motivation for moral uprightness is cultural evolution. Rabbi Jonathan Sacks, author of *The Great Partnership*, distinguishes cultural from biological evolution :

> Biological evolution favors individuals, but cultural evolution favors groups. Selfishness benefits individuals, but it is disastrous to groups, and it is only as members of a group that individuals can survive at all (Jacoby, 2013, p. A13).

Religion is part of culture, which he believes is "the only force strong enough to defeat egoism" (p. A13). Arguably this is an overstatement by Rabbi Sacks. Education is also a part of culture capable of imparting effective moral instruction. Psychologists William Kirk Kilpatrick, Thomas Lickona, Philip Zombardo, and Carl Rogers, psychiatrist Robert Coles, sociologist Samuel Oliner, and Rabbi Harold Kushner are among those who believe goodness can be taught.

A moving story in which community survival is prioritized over individual survival is found in Kay Jamison's bestselling memoir, *An Unquiet Mind*. There she recounts a jet pilot's decision to stay with his malfunctioning plane rather than bail out and survive. He knew that by parachuting he risked his unaccompanied plane crashing into a playground full of children. It is impossible to know if the pilot's heroic death was influenced by military training, religious education or the infusion of family values. What is undeniable is that he subordinated his survival to the survival of others.

Another moving story of self-sacrifice occurred on February 3, 1943 when the SS Dorchester, an American troop ship, was torpedoed by a German submarine. Six-hundred and seventy-four of the 904 men aboard were killed in the single greatest loss of life of any convoy during World War II. Included among the fatalities were Methodist preacher George Fox, Rabbi Alexander Goode, Catholic priest John Washington, and Reformed Church minister Clark Polling. In *The Pursuit of Happiness* psychologist David Myers provides this narrative:

> Within moments of a torpedo's impact, reports Lawrence Elliot, stunned men were pouring out from their bunks as the ship began listing. With power cut off, the escort vessels, unaware of the unfolding tragedy, pushed on in the darkness. On board, chaos

reigned as panicky men came up from the hold without life jackets and leaped into overcrowded lifeboats.

When the four chaplains made it up to the steeply sloping deck, they began guiding the men to their boat stations. They opened a storage locker, distributed life jackets, and coaxed the men over the side. In the icy, oily smeared water, Private William Bednar heard the chaplains preaching courage and found the strength to swim until he reached a life raft. Still on board, Grady Clark watched in awe as the chaplains handed out the last life jacket, and then, with ultimate selflessness, gave away their own. As Clark slipped into the waters he saw the chaplains standing – their arms linked – praying, in Latin, Hebrew, and English. Other men, now serene, joined them in a huddle as the Dorchester slid beneath the sea (1992, p. 196).

"Leave no man behind" is not an official military doctrine. It is an ethos embraced by combat soldiers calling for them to rescue their wounded comrades and recover those killed in action. Since fulfilling this credo exposes soldiers to danger it is reasonable to ask why it is important to retrieve soldiers who are not an asset to a mission. Journalist Charles Bausman offers this explanation:

While not captured in doctrine, there are few things more reassuring to a soldier about to enter combat than his brothers and sisters in arms would spare nothing in attempts to get him back. To the families of those fallen, the catharsis of being able to bury their own cannot be overstated or even understood by those who have not been in that sad and unfortunate position (2016, p. 3).

Combat requires a sense of obligation to teammates that far exceeds that of a football team. Soldiers in harm's way function optimally knowing they will be fully supported when taking risks. In his analysis of "Leave no man behind" Bausman concludes:

Ultimately, the responsibility lies with the commander on what he is willing to risk to ensure no man is left behind. It is a heavy burden, and may not be worth the loss of others in terms of mission accomplishment. These decisions are made in seconds, and will not be perfect. It is an unenviable position, and one he or she will undoubtedly debate for a lifetime (p. 4).

III. Why Are We the Only Moral Beings?

A man without ethics is a wild beast loosed upon the world.
- Albert Camus

The playwright Pierre-Augusten Caron Beaumarchais wrote, "Drinking when we are not thirsty and making love all year round, madam, that is all there is to distinguish us from other animals" (Malikow, 2013, p. 161). Beaumarchais' proposal is simplistic; there is more that distinguishes human beings from other animals than untimely drinking and seasonally unrestricted love-making. Making choices, imagining consequences, and being responsible make human beings unique in the pantheon of living things. As Mark Twain wryly observed, "Man is the only animal that blushes. Or needs to" (Negri, 1999, p. 1).

Only human beings have a responsibility to treat other animals humanely.

In *Consider the Lobster* David Foster Wallace invites the reader to consider whether lobsters experience pain when submerged in boiling water (2007). He suggests they might, thereby making eating lobster a moral issue. In 2007 professional football player Michael Vick was sentenced to 21 months in prison for the inhumane treatment of dogs as part of a dogfighting ring. The International Union for

Conservation of Nature has designated over 3,000 animals as *endangered species*, meaning they are vulnerable to extinction unless human beings cooperate in protective measures. Consider the following narrative from the ethics section of an introductory philosophy textbook:

Winchester, Massachusetts is a quaint little town located seven miles north of Boston. Its numerous colonial homes fronted by impeccably manicured lawns and charming town center contribute to Winchester being one of New England's priciest communities. Not that any town would have disregarded the invasion, but the pristine state of Winchester prior to the invasion made the intrusion especially troubling.

The invaders were Canada geese, a breed so large they walked about fearlessly with an air of entitlement. Hundreds of these geese deployed as dozens of flocks deposited cigar-sized droppings all over town, as if to mark their territory. A child licking an ice cream cone or eating a cookie near even one goose did so at risk.

When the undeniable became intolerable, a town meeting was called to address the problem. Subsequent meetings followed as each attempt to relocate the unwanted birds failed. Eventually came the meeting at which killing the geese was proposed and discussed. Advocates for extermination suggested paying hunters a bounty for each goose carcass. Those at the meeting who were outraged by this proposal made an impassioned argument that the birds, although bothersome and repugnant, had a right to live (Malikow, 2009, 13).

Those who argued the geese had an inviolable right to live believed the citizens of Winchester had an obligation to address the problem without killing the geese. Because of their size, Canada geese have few natural predators. However, they are a food source for coyotes, wolves, falcons, owls, and eagles; none of which have a moral obligation to restrain themselves from killing the geese. Only human beings would have a town meeting to discuss the morality of Canada geese extermination.

Only human beings commit suicide.

Evolutionary psychology asserts two fundamental human drives: survival and reproduction. If this is correct, human beings are no different from all other species. However, unlike all other organisms, human beings are capable of overriding the survival instinct and committing suicide. Even when some animals and insects seem to have committed suicide, they have not. Insect and animal self-sacrificial deaths are not suicides because they do not involve deliberation. These deaths are not self-determined but an innate reaction to a certain set of conditions. Thomas Joiner has elaborated on this phenomenon at length in his book, *Myths About Suicide*

(2011). Some aphids will explode when a wasp has deposited eggs inside the aphid for incubation. Similarly, Malaysian ants will explode as a final act of defense against nest invaders.

Self-detonating aphids and ants are fascinating as entomological phenomena, but neither is a moral issue. On the other hand, self-determined death by a human being is suitable for ethical discussion. The French sociologist Emile Durkheim classified suicide into four categories, one of which he designated altruistic suicide (1897). Self-sacrifice is the defining feature of this type of suicide. An altruistic suicide is a self-determined death motivated by what is perceived as a service to another person or persons. The previous chapter includes a reference to the altruistic suicide of the jet pilot in Kay Jamison's memoir, *An Unquiet Mind*. She describes her memory as one of the second graders on recess in the playground:

> I was standing with my head back, one pigtail caught between my teeth, listening to the jet overhead. The noise was loud, unusually so, which meant that it was close. My elementary school was near Andrews Air Force Base, just outside of Washington; many of us were pilots' kids, so the sound was a matter of routine. The noise of the jet became louder, and I saw the other children in my second-grade class dart their heads upward. The plane was coming in very low, then it streaked past us, scarcely missing the playground. As we stood there clumped together, it flew into the trees,

exploding directly in front of us. Over the next few days it became clear from the release of the young pilot's final message to the control tower before he died, that he knew he could save his own life by bailing out. He also knew, however, that by doing so he risked that his unaccompanied plane would fall onto the playground and kill those of us who were there.

The dead pilot became a hero, transformed into a scorchingly vivid, completely impossible ideal for what was meant by the concept of duty. The memory of the crash came back to me many times over the years, as a reminder both of how one aspires after and needs such ideals, and how killingly difficult it is to achieve them. I never again looked at the sky and saw only vastness and beauty. From that afternoon on I saw that death was also and always there (1995, pp. 11-13).

When a terminal, pain-riddled, fully cognizant patient requests a lethal injection from a physician, as occurred in 1998 when Thomas Youk appealed to Dr. Jack Kevorkian, a rational suicide is in progress . (Durkheim referred to these as fatalistic suicides.) Youk, age 52, was in the final stages of amyotrophic lateral sclerosis (a.k.a. Lou Gehrig's disease). Be it altruistic or rational, only a human being can engage in a premeditated, intentional, self-enacted death. This is not the case with aphids or ants (or lemmings or redback spiders or bumble bees). Even when soldiers obediently follow orders that take them to their death, they are acting from training, not instinct. This is what makes the calvary charge in Alfred Tennyson's poem "The Charge of the Light Brigade" heroic. These words are a celebration of bravery, not obtuseness:

Theirs not to make reply,
Theirs not to reason why,
Theirs but to do and die.
Into the valley of Death
Rode the six hundred (1854)

Only human beings have a conscience.

When Shakespeare wrote, "Conscience doth make cowards of us all" he was referring to the voice within that restrains dubious behavior (*Hamlet*, Act III, scene 1). Dr. Robert Hare, who conducted research on psychopaths for over twenty-five years, offers this definition of those who have no such inner voice:

(A psychopath) is a self-centered, callous, and remorseless person profoundly lacking in empathy and the ability to form warm emotional relationships with others, a person who functions without the restraints of conscience. (They) are lacking the very qualities that allow human beings live in social harmony (1999, p. 2).

A person lacking a conscience or whose conscience is blunted by disease or injury is a dangerously impaired human being. The word unconscionable literally means "unguided by conscience." Richard Kuklinski, possibly the most prolific serial murderer in American criminal history, said of himself, "I am what I am, and the truth is, I don't give a flying (expletive) what anyone thinks of me" (2003). Such indifference makes Kuklinski an avatar of Dr. Hare's definition. Only human beings can act unconscionably because only human beings have a conscience. Fortunately, according to Hare, psychopaths make up only one-percent of the general population.

If free will exists, only human beings have it.

Simply stated, free will is the ability to engage in authentic choice-making. While decision-making is always influenced by relevant factors, an influence is not an irresistible force. Aristotle affirmed free will when he asserted, "What it lies in our power to do, it lies also in our power not to do" (2014). Other advocates for free will posit without free will it would be impossible to hold people responsible for their behavior. Philosopher Thomas Ellis Katen characterizes free will as a defining feature of human beings:

> Which makes most sense of and best illustrates the facts of human experience as we know them? If the issue is put in these terms, I think the position could be developed that the idea of freedom is an inherent part of the defining concept of man (1973, p. 318).

In contrast to free will, *determinism* is the belief that human actions are not chosen but compelled by circumstances and conditioning. Supporting determinism is the law of cause-and-effect which assumes nothing is the cause of itself. In other words, everything that exists owes its existence to something prior to itself. (The only exception would be something that is eternal, if there is such a thing. Obviously, this is a metaphysical issue.) The French philosopher Paul Holbach believed, "every event is the necessary outcome of a cause or set of causes" (p. 313). He writes,

> Man's life is a line that nature commands him to describe upon the earth, without his ever being able to swerve from it even for an instant. Nevertheless, in spite of the shackles by which he is bound, it is pretended that he is a free agent (1770, p. 1).

The centuries old *free will vs. determinism debate* is relevant to moral philosophy because without free will there can be no moral decision-making. Without free will, every human action would be compelled by prior causes. This would mean just as insects and animals operate on instinct and bear no responsibility for anything they do, human beings would not be responsible for their actions since choice is an illusion.

Paraphrasing the 19th century German philosopher, Arthur Schopenhauer, a man can do what he desires, but he cannot choose what to desire. This thought allows for both authentic decision-making (free will) and the *law of cause-and-effect* (determinism). While people are not responsible for every thought and desire that occurs to them, they are responsible for managing thoughts and desires. Causation is not coercion. Human beings are not as animals and insects acting solely on instinct.

Conditions under which people are not responsible for their behavior.

On September 18, 1848 a Rutland and Burlington Railroad foreman named Phineas Gage had what is perhaps history's best-known industrial accident. An explosion drove a 3'7" iron rod through his head, entering under his left eye and exiting out of the top of his skull. Amazingly, Gage survived the ordeal, although he lost his left eye and suffered a partial facial paralysis. However, the most serious injury was to his brain. The passage of the rod severely damaged his left frontal cortex, the part of the brain responsible for impulse control. Until his death a dozen years later, Gage's behavior was unrestrained, given to fits of uncontrollable rage and rantings. It does not require an education in neurology to understand why Gage was not responsible for his volatile behavior.

In addition to a brain injury there are conditions under which people are not legally responsible for their behavior. In jurisprudence the standard for not guilty by reason of mental defect is the M'Naghten Rule. According to this rule the accused are not responsible for a criminal act if they are incapable of distinguishing "right" from "wrong" conduct or incapable of behaving in conformity to the law, even if they understand "right" and "wrong." Peter Carlquist, a psychiatric patient with paranoid schizophrenia, is an example of someone incapable of distinguishing "right" from "wrong." Several years ago, in full public view, he stabbed nine-year-old Katie Mason to death (Nuland, 1993, p. 124). An example of someone incapable of conforming her behavior to the law in spite of a knowledge of "right" and "wrong" is Andrea Yates. In a highly publicized case she drowned her five children, ranging in age from seven years to six months, in a bathtub and then called the police to surrender herself. Her psychiatric diagnosis was postpartum depression and postpartum psychosis. Found not guilty by reason of mental defect, she remains confined in a psychiatric facility.

A third legal category by which an individual is not responsible for a crime is acting on an irresistible impulse. Commonly referred to as a "crime of passion" and "temporary insanity," an irresistible impulse arises under extraordinary conditions. An example from fiction is John Grisham's novel, *A Time to Kill* (1989), in which a father murders two men who raped and maimed his ten year-old daughter. (Grisham's novel was inspired by an actual case he witnessed in a Mississippi courtroom.)

In actual practice, determining responsibility for a criminal act is sometimes complicated by the *law of unintended consequences*. People who do not have diminished capacity as determined by the M'Naghten Rule might still be fully responsible for a criminal act. A person driving while intoxicated (DWI) who causes an automobile accident is fully responsible for the accident. If the accident caused a death (not the driver's) this would be an unintended consequence. Since this consequence was foreseeable the intoxicated driver is also responsible for the death.

Determining responsibility for an accident that occurred on April 23, 2006 in Upstate New York is not as obvious. On that day State Trooper Craig Todeschini was killed when he lost control of his vehicle pursuing James Carncross, who was on a motorcycle evading the trooper at speeds in excess of 100 miles per hour. Carncross was found guilty of criminally negligent homicide and sentenced to eight years in prison. His trial raised the question of what constitutes foreseeability. It is one thing to say people are responsible for their actions. It is another to say they are responsible for every event in a sequence that was initiated by something they did. While people are responsible for all foreseeable events that follow their actions and are connected to them there is no formula for distinguishing foreseeable from unforeseeable events. At trial Carncross' attorney argued it is unreasonable to assume Trooper Todeschini's death was foreseeable to Carncross. Before attempting his escape, if he considered the possibilities, they would have included getting caught, getting away, or getting himself killed. Todeschini's death was not considered a possibility because it was not foreseeable. Carncross took for granted the trooper's ability to take care of himself. This is not to assert Carncross is not guilty of anything. His case is offered to illustrate the difficulty of assigning responsibility when an unintended consequence has occurred.

Only human beings are capable of evil.

William James, who made noteworthy contributions to philosophy and psychology, elegantly expressed the capacity of human beings for evil as well as good.

> Surely there is no status for good and evil to exist in a purely insentient world. The moment one sentient being, however, is made part of the universe, there is a chance for goods and evils really to exist" (1891, p. 7).

The Greek word translated as "evil" is *poneros*, defined as, "deliberate defiance of the moral law without regard to the pain and suffering brought to others by such defiance" (Thayer, 1996). It is not surprising that Hare's consummate work on psychopaths is titled *Without Conscience* (1999). There are innumerable sources of pain and suffering in this world - earthquakes, tsunamis, hurricanes, tornados, disease, birth defects, and predatory creatures – none of which require human agency. Even the COVID-19 virus, the cause of worldwide disruption and hundreds of thousands of deaths, is not spoken of as evil. In contrast, the Holocaust, My Lai Massacre, murders, rapes, and child abductions all require at least one human being acting in defiance of the moral law without regard to the resulting pain and suffering. Evil is exclusively the work of human beings, making the expression "human evil" a redundancy. Only human beings can deliberate on their behavior, calculate its consequences, and decide whether to proceed or desist. When the decision is made to proceed in spite of painful consequences for others evil is the word to describe such behavior.

It is not unusual to speak of someone's behavior as bad; it is quite another to speak of someone as an evil person. Evil is an adjective reserved for the infamous few like Adolf Hitler, Richard Kuklinski, and Josef Stalin. However, a case can be made for evil behavior as within the scope of virtually everyone. The philosopher Adam Morton devotes an entire book to making this argument. In the introduction to *On Evil* he writes,

> We're in the midst of it as always. Human beings are committing atrocities on one another with the same enthusiasm or carelessness that has always marked our species. When we think of evil we first think of large scale horrors. But by the end of this book I hope to have convinced you that most evil acts are performed by people disturbingly like you and me ... (2004, pp. Ix-x).

A contemporary philosopher, Sam Harris, agrees and writes,

> I also believe that most of the evil in our world – all the needless misery we manufacture for one another –

is the product, not of what bad people do, but of what good people do once in the grip of bad ideas. there is no telling how much moral progress we might make by removing the impediments to clear thinking on any topic that interests us (2020, p. xi).

One of best known investigations in the history of psychology is Stanley Milgram's study of obedience and compliance. In a brilliantly constructed and controversial experiment, Professor Milgram purposed to understand the submission to authority that made the Holocaust possible. He was curious about the capacity of people for following orders that require the administration of pain on others. In his words, "I set up a simple experiment at Yale University to test how much pain an ordinary citizen would inflict on another person simply because he was ordered by an experimental psychologist (1963, p. 371). Presented as a learning experiment, the target subject was told that he would be a "teacher" who would be asking questions to a "learner." The teacher was told the source of the questions would be material the learner had previously studied. The teacher was further instructed to administer an electrical shock to the learner when an incorrect answer was given. The teacher and learner would be in different rooms and communicate by way of an intercom. A panel on the teacher's desk had levers that would send shocks to the learner when pulled. The shocks ranged from ten to 450 volts in increments of ten. The voltage sent to the learner would increase with each additional incorrect response. The experimenter lied to the teacher. The experiment was not a study of the effect of pain on recall. Actually, there would be no shocks and the learner would feign being in pain, eventually crying out and begging for the experiment to stop. The study was intended to observe if the teachers would continue to administer shocks after the learners were expressing intense pain and possibly injury.

The only real shock in this experiment was the one experienced by Milgram. He estimated that few of the teachers would continue in the experiment after the learner communicated extreme pain. Instead, 65 percent of the teachers inflicted the full 450 volts on the learners and none of the teachers stopped before 300 volts. As long as the experimental psychologist provided reassurance that he would take full responsibility for any injury to the learner, the teachers continued to ask questions and pull levers.

As far as can be known, only human beings can display virtue.

Some animals engage in behavior that human beings evaluate as virtue. The dog who protects a family from an intruder seems courageous. The mother cat that accepts an orphaned baby rabbit as part of her litter seems charitable. The elephant herd that surrounds the body of one of its deceased elders seems respectful. Does moral excellence require a choice? If it does then until the inner workings of animals are known the question of whether they are acting courageously, charitably or respectfully cannot be answered.

IV. How Should We Determine Right and Wrong?

Always behave in such a way that you'll never be ashamed of the truth about yourself.

- Fred "Mister" Rogers

Deciding on the title of this chapter came with some difficulty. The other contender was "How Do We Determine Right from Wrong?" Some of the philosophers in this chapter address how people arrive at moral decisions. Other contributors insist on the way in which moral decisions should be made. The agenda for this chapter is to present both the practices by which moral decisions are made and the prescriptions advocated by six philosophers and one psychiatrist. David Hume and Robert Coles address how people make moral decisions. Immanuel Kant, Jeremy Bentham, John Stuart Mill, Simone deBeauvoir, and Joseph Fletcher offer the prescriptions for moral decision-making.

The following moral dilemma, created by psychologist Jonathan Haidt, provides an opportunity to consider the basis upon which certain behaviors are considered immoral.

Julie and Mark are brother and sister. They are traveling together in France on summer vacation from college. One night they are staying alone together in a cabin near the beach. They decide it would be very

interesting and fun if they tried making love. At the
very least, it would be a new experience for each of
them. Julie was already taking birth control pills, but
Mark uses a condom too, just to be safe. They both
enjoy making love, but they decide to never do it
again. They keep that night as a special secret, which
makes them feel even closer to each other. What do
you think about that? Was it o.k. for them to make
love? (2006, pp. 20-21)

If you believe Julie and Mark acted immorally, on what do
you base your judgment? It cannot be on practical grounds,
since neither a sexually transmitted disease nor a pregnancy
was a possibility. If you believe it was illegal the laws against
incest vary from country to country and from state to state
within the United States. Moreover, a conviction would
require a confession by either Mark or Julie and probably both
of them. If you consider their sexual experiment immoral, this
would raise the question, "Whose morality?" The Hebrew
Bible forbids various forms of incest (Leviticus 18:8-18;
20:11-21) and the New Testament denounces a case of
intrafamilial sex in one of the Pauline epistles (1Corinthians
5:1-5). If the biblical prohibition of incest is understood as
God's way of preventing birth defects then the religious
prohibition is actually rooted in a practical consideration. This
would mean if no pregnancy could occur, as with Julie and
Mark, then arguably there is nothing wrong with their
lovemaking. Over centuries, philosophers, theologians, and

psychologists have offered suggestions and explanations for moral decision-making.

Divine Inspiration

Immanuel Kant believed humankind exists in the subjective, physical realm (*phenomena*) without access to the objective, nonphysical domain (*noumena*), inhabited by God. Kant did note one exception, that being the conscience, which God provides so human beings would have a sense of how they ought to live. Kant's understanding of the conscience moved him to write, "In law a man is guilty when he violates the rights of others. In ethics he is guilty if he only thinks of doing so" (2014).

Kant further believed since moral precepts derive from God, they are to be followed without exception, making them absolute. Kant's approach to ethics is deontological, derived from the Greek word *deon*, which means duty. The idea that right and wrong vary from person to person, situation to situation, culture to culture or era to era was an abomination to Kant. In his *Grounding for the Metaphysics of Morals* (1785) he used the term "categorical imperatives" to refer to the principles of conduct that are to be followed regardless of circumstances. Three of these imperatives are *universalization, human dignity*, and *reciprocity*. Universalization guides moral conduct by asking: Would the world be a better place if everyone acted as you are about to act? Human dignity asserts never are people to be employed as a means to an end because nothing is more important than a human being. Reciprocity asks: If you were a king who could decree the laws by which others would have to live, would you be willing to live under those laws?

Sentimentalism

In common parlance sentimental refers to someone who is excessively prone to feelings of tenderness, sadness or nostalgia. This understanding also applies to sentimentalism in moral philosophy, meaning right and wrong exist as feelings rather than precepts. The well-known conundrum of whether there is noise when a tree falls in an unpopulated forest is parallel to whether right and wrong exist as entities apart from human experience. Sentimentalists like David Hume maintain right and wrong do not exist until someone has a feeling about an event or circumstance.

A fascinating experiment conducted by British psychology professor Bruce Hood provides a striking example of the human proclivity to make choices based on sentiment rather than reason. In his investigation, he offered student subjects 10 pounds (approximately $15) if they would wear a sweater he held before them. Nearly everyone agreed until he told them the cardigan once belonged to Fred West, a notorious serial murderer who had abducted and killed a dozen women. After being informed of the sweater's previous owner, nearly everyone who had agreed to wear the sweater then refused to do so. When asked to explain their change of mind, none of the participants could offer a rational explanation. Instead, in various ways, each said, "I just don't want that on my body." Such an explanation is reminiscent of Blaise Pascal's assessment: "The heart has its reasons of which reason knows nothing" (2014).

In *A Treatise of Human Nature* (1740) Hume characterized reason as enslaved to passion and completely impotent in moral decision-making, serving only an advisory role in moral deliberations. It's difficult to disagree with him given the frequency with which people admit to having acted contrarily to reason. A well-publicized survival story supports Hume's assertion that passion trumps other factors when contemplating a moral act. In 1972 a plane carrying a Uruguayan rugby team crashed in the Andes Mountains, killing 29 of the 45 passengers. Some of the 16 survivors resorted to cannibalism in order to stay alive. They felt survival justified eating from the bodies of the deceased. Those who refused to eat from the dead felt doing so would be morally wrong. For both groups the decision was made on the basis of feeling. Some of the survivors felt it was right to prioritize survival over cannibalism and others felt even survival did not justify eating flesh from corpses.

Remarkable is the agreement between Hume, an 18th century philosopher, and Sapolksy, a 21st century neuroscientist. In a conversation with Sam Harris, Sapolsky said,

We assume that as creatures with big cortexes, reason is at the core of most of our decision making. And an awful lot of work has shown that far more often than we'd like to think, we make our decisions based on implicit, autonomic reflexes. We make them within milliseconds. Parts of the brain that are marinated in emotion and hormones are activating long, long before the more cortical rational parts activate.

And often what we believe is rational thinking is, instead, our cognitive selves playing catch-up, trying to rationalize the notion that our emotional instincts are perfectly logical and make wonderful sense (Harris, 2020, p. 259).

This agreement is echoed by Haidt in his analysis of political disagreements:

Moral intuitions arise automatically and almost instantly, long before moral reasoning has a chance to get started, and those first intuitions tend to drive our later reasoning Keep your eye on intuitions, and don't take people's moral arguments at face value. They are mostly post hoc constructions made up on the fly, crafted to advance one or more strategic objectives (2012, p. xx).

Utilitarianism

Jeremy Bentham encapsulated utilitarianism when he wrote, "The greatest happiness of the greatest number is the foundation of morals and legislation" (2014). As an approach to moral philosophy, utilitarianism is teleological and consequential. It is teleological because the end is identified ("the greatest happiness") and consequential because a good result justifies the action (happiness being the good result). For the utilitarian, an action is morally right if it produces the greatest possible happiness for the greatest number of involved people and/or the most favorable balance of pleasure over pain. Utilitarians rhetorically ask, "How could something not be good if it produces good?"

Utilitarianism has appeal in a democratic society owing to its deference to the majority. Further, it stresses impartiality in that everyone's happiness counts the same. Another utilitarian, John Stuart Mill, addressed the good of the majority and impartiality with these words: "The only freedom which deserves the name is that of pursuing our own good, in our own way, so long as we do not attempt to deprive others of theirs, or impede their efforts to obtain it" (2014).

Utilitarianism is not without its critics. Hume questioned it on the ground that neither the "greatest good" nor the "greatest number" can be calibrated. A consideration of the atomic bombings of Hiroshima and Nagasaki in World War II elucidates Hume's argument against utilitarianism. President Harry S. Truman defended his decision to use the ultimate weapon of that time with this statement:

Having found the bomb we have used it. We have used it against those who attacked us without warning at Pearl Harbor, against those who have starved and beaten and executed American prisoners of war, against those who have abandoned all pretense of obeying international laws of warfare. We have used it in order to shorten the agony of war, in order to save the lives of thousands and thousands of young Americans. We will continue to use it until we completely destroy Japan's power to make war. Only a Japanese surrender will stop us. When you have to deal with a beast, you have to treat him as a beast. It is most regrettable but nevertheless true (08/06/1945).

His argument is irrefutable if the consequences are limited to the "greatest good" of the United States. However, his decision is vulnerable to criticism if the "greatest good" is expanded to include the estimated 150,000 Japanese civilians killed in the two bombings. Moreover, the well-known axiom, "All is fair in love and war," notwithstanding, the 1949 Geneva Convention reaffirmed and formalized the understanding that lethal action against noncombatants is unethical.

Situational Ethics/Relativism

The name Joseph Fletcher is virtually synonymous with situational ethics, largely due to his controversial book,

Situational Ethics: The New Morality (1966). An ordained Episcopal minister and seminary professor, he eventually declared himself an atheist. Nevertheless, he agreed with the biblical precept, "Love thy neighbor" (Mark 12:31, *King James Bible*) and wrote, "Love wills the neighbor's good, whether we like him or not" (1966, p. 120).

Situational ethics is a relativistic approach to morality because it asserts there are no moral absolutes. Hence, an action that is morally wrong in one situation can be morally right in another. For Fletcher, the guiding principle for moral conduct is *agape*, the Greek word for "unselfish, outgoing affection or tenderness for another without necessarily expecting anything in return" (Hill, 1987, p. 538). Among his controversial views are the moral rightness of abortion, euthanasia, and suicide if they are motivated by love. He argued absolute, abstract laws of morality are meaningless and must give way to the most loving action in a given situation. In fact, Fletcher saw love as the defining characteristic of morality: "We ought to love people and use things; the essence of immorality is to love things and use people" (2014). Accordingly, he believed an action acquires the status of moral rightness when it is the most loving thing to do. A striking illustration of situational ethics is found in John Steinbeck's classic novel *Of Mice and Men*. Under normal circumstances the thought of fatally shooting an unarmed, unsuspecting man is reprehensible. However, the story ends with George shooting Lenny, a mentally retarded gentle giant. Literally not knowing his own strength, Lenny unintentionally kills a woman. Rather than have Lenny face the cruelty of the posse closing in on him and either life imprisonment or execution, George shoots Lenny as an act of compassion.

Obedience to Authority

The renown psychiatrist M. Scott Peck has written, "Triggers are pulled by individuals. Orders are given and executed by individuals. In the last analysis, every single human act is ultimately the result of an individual choice" (1983, p. 215). What are the possibilities when individuals believe they are not responsible for their actions? The aforementioned Milgram experiment (Chapter III) provides the answer. Recall that 65 percent of the administering subjects continued shocking up to what they believed to be the maximum voltage (450 volts). Reflecting on his study 13 years later, Milgram writes:

> Ordinary people, simply doing their jobs, and without any particular hostility on their part, can become agents in a terrible destructive process. Moreover, even when the destructive effects of their work become patently clear, and they are asked to carry out actions incompatible with fundamental standards of morality, relatively few people have the resources needed to resist authority.

One explanation for morality succumbing to obedience is the relief of responsibility that occurs when an authority figure provides assurance that those being ordered will not be responsible for any unfavorable consequences.

While the results of Milgram's study are indeed disheartening, some comfort can be taken in knowing it was merely an experiment. Unfortunately, this is not the case with the My Lai Massacre, the Vietnam War's darkest hour. On the morning of March 16, 1968, American ground troops moved into a small group of hamlets in South Vietnam known collectively as My Lai. What followed is not entirely clear. What is known with certainty is somewhere between 350 and 500 unarmed, noncombatant villagers were shot to death in various ways. In the ensuing investigation the soldiers maintained they were merely following orders. Peck, chairman of the psychiatric committee that investigated My Lai, writes:

> It is an old maxim that soldiers are not supposed to think. Leaders are not elected from within a group but are designated from above and deliberately cloaked in the symbols of authority. Obedience is the number-one military discipline. The dependency of the soldier on his leader is not simply encouraged, it is mandated.
>
> In situations such as My Lai, the individual soldier is in an almost impossible situation. On one hand, he may vaguely remember being told in some classroom that he is not required to forsake his conscience and should have the mature independence of judgment -

even the duty - to refuse to obey an illegal order. On the other hand, the military organization and its group dynamics do everything to make it just about as painful and difficult and unnatural as possible for the soldier to exercise independence of judgment or practice disobedience (1983, p. 224).

The Free Will of Others

The existential philosopher and novelist Simone de Beauvoir provided a different guiding principle for moral conduct: act to maximize the freedom of others. She maintained since our values are largely expressed by our behavior toward others, it is through relationships that we disclose who we are. "To will oneself free is also to will others free" expresses her belief that the guiding principle in our relationships should be acting to maximize the freedom of others as well as holding them responsible for their actions (1954, p. 73).

> She emphasized since we cannot completely know what the results of our choices will be, we can never be certain an action is right while contemplating it. However, although we cannot know the specific outcome of a choice, we can accurately estimate whether that choice will contribute to our own or another person's freedom. Hence, a corollary to her

guiding principle is treating others as we ourselves would desire to be treated (Malikow, 2014, pp. 44-45).

An extreme expression of de Beauvoir's principle is found in the writing of the antinatalist David Benatar. (An antinatalist is one who believes it is immoral to procreate.) Benatar's rationale for antinatalism is presented in his controversial book *Better Never to Have Been: The Harm of Coming into Existence* (2006). He believes the pleasures that await the unborn are far outweighed by the pain in store for them. Moreover, since the unborn have no choice concerning their existence, they have no opportunity to exercise free will in life's most important question: "To be or not to be?" (*Hamlet*, Act III, scene 1). Therefore, the decision to bring a human being into existence goes beyond minimizing the freedom of another; it eliminates it altogether. Benatar writes, "I am under no illusions. My position, no matter how clearly stated, is likely to be misunderstood" (2012, p. 16). Actually, although his position is easily understood, it is nevertheless controversial. The polemic derives from antinatalism being counterintuitive to the human instincts for survival and reproduction.

Education and Nurturing

In the fall of 1960 a six-year-old girl named Ruby Bridges entered the William Frantz Elementary School in New Orleans, Louisiana. She was accompanied by United States

Marshals, assigned for her safety. She was the first black child to attend this previously all-white school. Ruby's groundbreaking entrance did not go unnoticed. In addition to the protesting crowd threatening and taunting her were an artist and a psychiatrist. The artist was Norman Rockwell and the psychiatrist was Robert Coles. One of Rockwell's most familiar drawings is that of Ruby Bridges accompanied by her protectors. One of Robert Coles' many books is *The Story of Ruby Bridges* (1995).

Can goodness be taught? The answer to this question is a resounding "yes" according to several academics who have given considerable attention to this question. In addition to Dr. Coles are Samuel Oliner, a sociologist and Holocaust survivor, William Kirk Kilpatrick, a psychologist and author, and Philip Zimbardo, a researcher well-known for his Stanford Prisoners Experiment. Each believes a child can be nurtured into human decency by education and personal encounters. Coles, who investigated the moral lives of children for over fifty years, has provided a manual for parents and teachers entitled *How to Raise a Moral Child* (1998).

Responsibility

Existentialism is the philosophical movement derived from and emphasizing free will and personal responsibility. Its earliest expression as a distinct school of thought are the 19th century writings of Soren Kierkegaard and Friedrich Nietzsche. Prominent 20th century existential voices are those of Martin Heidegger, Jean-Paul Sartre, and Albert Camus. In his ironic statement, "Man is condemned to be free," Sartre expressed his belief that people fear their own freedom (1957, p. 23). He maintained human beings have free will and with it comes complete responsibility for their actions and the consequences of their actions. "Man is condemned to be free" because there is no escape from this responsibility.

Sartre further believed such responsibility is intimidating to many people. Nietzsche is well-known for his declaration, "God is dead" (1974, p. 95). Nietzsche recognized without God or some other absolute moral authority over humankind there is moral anarchy. "Nevertheless, he saw something redemptive emerging from this moral chaos: each of us bears responsibility for constructing and living out a self-determined morality" (Malikow, 2014, p. 16). Nietzsche also believed in two fundamental moralities: "There is a master morality and a slave morality" (1966, p. 260). Those with a slave morality submit to a religion or some other moral authority in order to evade responsibility for their behavior. These people justify their behavior by saying, "I was merely following orders." In contrast, those with a master morality unflinchingly accept responsibility for their conduct because it is guided by their self-constructed moral code.

V. Why Do We Make Morally Wrong Decisions?

On the whole, human beings want to be good, but not too good, and not quite all the time.

- George Orwell

Human beings are a species splendid in their array of moral equipment, tragic in their propensity to misuse it, and pathetic in their constitutional ignorance of the misuse.

- Robert Wright

In the New Testament the Apostle Paul writes of himself,

> I do not understand what I do. For what I want to do I do not do, but what I hate I do. For I have the desire to do what is good, but I cannot carry it out. For what I do is not the good I want to do; no, the evil I do not want to do – this I keep on doing (Romans 7: 15, 18-19).

If the human instrument for writing one-fourth of the New Testament confessed to frustration at his inability to live in accordance with his moral code then what does this imply about the rest of us? Paul said he did not understand why he persisted in this failure. This chapter offers 11 reasons why we make morally wrong decisions.

Ignorance

Socrates believed we engage in wrongdoing unaware of the harm we are doing to ourselves. He reasoned since we do not seek to harm to ourselves it follows that misconduct results from our ignorance of the harm we are self-inflicting. When we lack this awareness we behave immorally.

The misbehavior of addiction provides an example of Socrates' view. Stanton Peele, a psychologist and expert on addiction, has characterized the world of an addict as continually shrinking. Over time, as the addiction increasingly claims more of the addict's life, time and attention given to activities and responsibilities unrelated to the addiction diminish until they virtually disappear. Eventually the addict's life is reduced to two entities – the addict and servicing the addiction. Socrates would submit if the addict understood this shrinkage the addictive process would not continue. Obviously, his analysis does not address those who misbehave with full awareness of the harm they are doing to themselves. If cigarette smoking can be considered a form of misconduct it is invalid to argue that cigarette smokers persist in their habit because they are unaware of the harm they are doing to themselves.

Failure to Habituate

"Watch your thoughts, they become your words; watch your words, they become your actions; watch your actions, they become your habits; watch your habits, they become your character; watch your character, it becomes your destiny."

This progression is attributed to Lao-Tzu, an ancient Chinese philosopher. (It's also been attributed to Mahatma Gandhi and Margaret Thatcher.) Whoever said it agrees with Will Durant's analysis of moral excellence. (Also attributed to Aristotle):

> Excellence is an art won by training and habituation. We do not act rightly because we have virtue or excellence, but we rather have those because we have acted rightly. We are what we repeatedly do. Excellence, then, is not an act but a habit (1926, p. 98).

Shakespeare also understood the dynamic of habituation. In *The Tragedy of Hamlet, Prince of Denmark*, Hamlet appeals to his mother, Gertrude, to make a significant change in her life.

> Assume a virtue if you have it not.
> Refrain tonight.
> And that shall lend a kind of easiness
> To the next abstinence; the next more easy
> For use can almost change the stamp of nature
> (Act III. scene 4).

Miscalculation

Closely related to ignorance is miscalculation. We don't have to advance very far in life before reflecting on a misdeed with, "If only I had known then what I know now." (Or, as

Bob Seger reflected in song, "Wish I didn't know now what I didn't know then" [1980].) One understanding of sin is to view it as an attempt to get a good thing in a bad way. Pain relief is a good thing, but addiction to Oxycontin is not. Relief from the depression and ennui of a devitalized marriage is a good thing, but an extramarital affair is not. Concerning infidelity, Francesca Johnson, a character in Robert Waller's classic novel *The Bridges of Madison County*, accurately calculates the consequences of abandoning her family by running off with Robert Kincaid, her lover. She explains to him her decision not to go:

> As much as I want you and want to be with you and part of you, I can't tear myself away from the realness of my responsibilities. Don't make me give this up, my responsibilities. I cannot do that and live with the thought of it. If I did leave now, those thoughts would turn me into something other than the woman you have come to love.
>
> Robert Kincaid was silent. He knew what she was saying about the road and responsibilities and how the guilt could transform her. He knew she was right, in a way (1992, p. 116).

In contrast to Francesca is boxing legend Muhammed Ali's reflection on his years of womanizing and adultery:

I used to chase women all the time. And I won't say I was right, but look at all the temptations I had. I was young, handsome, heavyweight champion of the world. Women were always offering themselves to me. I had two children by women I wasn't married to. I love them; they're my children. I feel just as good and proud of them as I do my other children, but it wasn't the right thing to do. And running around, living that kind of life, wasn't good for me. It hurt my wife, it offended God. It never really made me happy. But ask any man who's forty years old – if he knew at twenty what he knows now, would he do things different? Most people would. So I did wrong; I'm sorry. And all I'll say as far as running around chasing women is concerned, is that's all past. I've got a good wife now, and I'm lucky to have her (Hauser, 1991, p. 310).

Rationalization

Recall Robert Heilein's observation that, "Man is not a rational animal, he is a rationalizing animal" (2005, p. 542). Concerning rationalization, Muel Kaplein, a professor of business ethics, writes,

When people's actions differ from their morals, they begin to rationalize both to protect themselves from a painful contradiction and to build up protection against accusations. The bigger the dissonance, the larger the rationalization, and the longer it lasts, the less immoral it seems (Martin, 2016).

Lieutenant William Calley, part of the chain of command at the aforementioned My Lai Massacre, rationalized his participation at his trial in 1970:

> I was ordered to go up there and destroy the enemy. That was my job that day. That was the mission I was given. I did not sit down and think about men, women, and children. They were all classified as the same, and that was the classification we dealt with over there, just as the enemy. I felt then and I still do that I acted as I was directed, and I carried out the order that I was given and I do not feel wrong in doing so (2015).

It should be noted that nearly 40 years after his trial, Calley publicly expressed regret over following that order:

> There is not a day that goes by that I do not feel remorse for what happened that day at My Lai. I feel remorse for the Vietnamese who were killed, for their families, for the American soldiers involved and their families. I am very sorry. If you are asking why I did not stand up to them when I was given the orders, I will have to say that I was a 2nd Lieutenant getting orders from my commander and I followed them – foolishly, I guess (Nix, 2009).

Brain Injury and Mental Health Disorders

Phineas Gage, presented in chapter II, is perhaps the best-known example of someone not responsible for his behavior owing to a brain injury. (Recall that he had an iron rod pass through his brain.) Most instances of misconduct explained by brain pathology are not as stunning or obvious as Gage's. Arthur Shawcross, the "Genessee River Killer," convicted of ten murders and sentenced to 250 years in prison in 1990, was examined by forensic psychiatrist Dorothy Lewis. She testified for the defense at his trial and presented a neurological explanation for his psychopathic behavior based on magnetic resonance imaging (MRI):

> The MRI had shown that, nestled at the tip of his right temporal lobe, was a small, fluid-filled cyst. The brain is a very sensitive organ. The tiniest scar or tumor or cyst can, under certain circumstances, trigger abnormal electrical activity. Abnormal electrical foci at the anterior pole of the temporal lobe have been associated with bizarre, animalistic behaviors (1998, p. 272).

Dr. Lewis' testimony did not influence the jury. Moreover, she was reviled by the media and public. Instead of being respected as a scientist and expert, she was maligned as being effusively sympathetic to a serial murderer:

Not only did the jury not believe me, they hated me. Then again, so did the rest of Rochester (New York). Night after night during the course of my testimony I would return to my hotel room I would then switch on the news and watch the man (or woman) in the street belittle me and my testimony.It was a nightmare (p. 280).

The case of Charles Whitman is similar to that of Shawcross. On August 1, 1966 he went on a shooting spree after fatally stabbing his wife and mother. He opened fire from the observation deck of the Administration Building of the University of Texas at Austin killing 16 and wounding 32 before being fatally shot by police officers. A letter found in his apartment after these events reads:

I really don't understand myself these days ... Lately I have been a victim of many unusual and irrational thoughts. These thoughts constantly recur and it requires tremendous mental effort to concentrate on useful and progressive tasks. After my death I wish that an autopsy be performed to see if there is any visible physical disorder. I have had tremendous headaches in the past and have consumed two large bottles of Excedrin in the past three months (1966).

The autopsy performed on Whitman showed a glioblastoma in his brain, an aggressive cancer that compromises the ability to control emotions and actions.

The research of Robert Hare, referred to in chapter III, suggests psychopaths have abnormal brain wave patterns. When he submitted the results of a study of psychopaths to a scientific journal it was rejected by its editor with the explanation, "Frankly, we found some of the brain wave patterns depicted in the paper very odd. Those EEG's (electroencephalograms) couldn't have come from real people" (Hare, 1999, p. 1). Hare admits to the brain wave patterns being very odd but the EEG's had been gathered from a group of real people known as psychopaths.

Peter Carlquist, the man with schizophrenia who publicly murdered a little girl, and Andrea Yates, the psychotic woman who drowned her five children, are offered in chapter III as examples of "not guilty by reason of mental defect." They also serve as examples of homicides attributable to a brain disease. The same might be said of a character in an Edgar Allen Poe short story. In *The Black Cat* a deeply disturbed man attributes his homicidal behavior to the disease of alcohol. Before murdering his wife he enucleated and then hanged his cat. He offers as an explanation,

> I slipped a noose around its neck and hung it to the limb of a tree; - hung it with the tears streaming from my eyes; and with the bitterest remorse in my heart; - hung it because I knew that it had loved me, and

because I felt it had given me no reason for offence; - hung it because I knew that in so doing I was committing a sin – a deadly sin that would so jeopardize my immortal soul as to place it – if such were possible – even beyond the reach of the infinite mercy of the Most Merciful and Most Terrible God (2016, p. 9).

Failure to Respect the Free Will of Others

Sam Harris believes, with few exceptions, it is morally wrong to lie because,

> by lying, we deny others our view of the world. And our dishonesty not only influences the choices they make, it often determines the choices they can make – in ways we cannot always predict. Every lie is an assault on the autonomy of those we lie to (2013, p. 41).

This statement implies that lying impairs the exercise of free will, which is true if we have free will. But Harris also writes,

> I'm often taken in by the illusion of agency. Often, my emotional response to bad actions in the world makes sense only if I'm viewing people as real agents, as the authors of their actions. Whether the universe is purely

deterministic or there's an added factor of randomness doesn't matter; that still gives us no basis to believe in free will. Every person is a puppet who didn't pick his own strings, and the strings reach back to the Big Bang (2020, p. 270).

This apparent discrepancy notwithstanding, other great thinkers (I consider Harris a great thinker) believe it is immoral to diminish the authentic choice-making of others. Simone de Beauvoir and David Benatar, referred to in the previous chapter, are among those who believe a failure to respect the free will of others constitutes an immoral act.

Deflection of Responsibility

Deflect is a verb meaning to turn something away from its direct course. Applied to psychology, deflecting is a defense mechanism we use to direct blame away from ourselves toward someone or something else. It's employed unconsciously to make us feel less bad about our wrongdoings.

Stanley Milgram's obedience and compliance experiment, described in chapter III, provides an exceptional example of deflection of responsibility. As long as the experimental psychologist provided reassurance that he would take full responsibility for any injury to the learner, the teachers continued to ask questions and administer electrical shocks. After the experiment, when asked how they were able to continue dispensing shocks up to the maximum voltage to subjects who were crying out in pain, they responded that it was the supervising psychologist's responsibility to stop the experiment.

Dispersion of Responsibility

Several writers have said, "No snowflake in an avalanche ever feels responsible." (This has been attributed to the poet Stanislaw Jerzy Lec and philosopher Voltaire among others.) In his analysis of the Holocaust, Rabbi Dr. Richard Rubenstein explained the system that made the Holocaust possible in terms of a dispersion of responsibility. He posited the deaths of millions of Jews required thousands of executioners. However, the division of labor that made this genocide possible also made most of the executioners unaware of their contribution to the project. The killing of six million people involved so many steps divided among so many people that the perpetrators became as snowflakes in an avalanche.

Fear

Edmund Burke understood that fear drives much wrongdoing and wrote, "No passion so effectually robs the mind of all its powers of acting and reasoning as *fear*" (2015, p. 47). Fear of discovery explains why a manageable problem is often exceeded by an attempt to hide it. Presidents Nixon and Clinton provide historical examples of the coverup being worse than the crime. Fear of failure accounts for cheating on a test or misrepresenting research data. And fear of death can motivate behavior that is antithetical to the military code, "Death before dishonor." The Kapos in the Nazi concentration camps were prisoners who were given supervisory responsibilities over other prisoners and received special privileges, including release from hard labor. They chose betrayal of their people in order to survive.

Entitlement

The leader had soared to prominence, catapulting from one job to the next, winning support from people who shared his beliefs, admired his style and saw in him a certain benevolent power. He seemed to relish the crowds, yet he had a striking ability to connect with an individual. And then he fell, unable to restrain his lust (Fisher, 1998).

This is a description of Gordon MacDonald, the minister who served as Bill Clinton's spiritual advisor in the wake of the President's moral failure – a moral failure he shared with MacDonald. In 1987 anonymous letters to MacDonald's religious publishers revealed his extramarital affair three years earlier. His restoration to ministry included two years of a carefully orchestrated regimen of reflection, counseling, and accountability. One of the insights he acquired in those years was how a misguided sense of entitlement contributed to his moral dereliction. He realized he had rationalized the considerable good he was doing as a pastor, author, and conference speaker entitled him to a secretive indulgence. Muel Kaplein could have had Gordon MacDonald in mind when he wrote: "Sometimes people, having been moral and forthright in their dealings for a long time, feel as if they have banked up some kind of 'ethical credit,' which they may use to justify immoral behavior in the future" (Martin, 2016).

Anonymity

The mythical Ring of Gyges, referred to in chapter II, provides anonymity to its wearers by making them invisible. Although the ubiquitousness of surveillance cameras and cell phones have made anonymity harder to acquire, a feeling of invisibility can come from being part of a crowd. Social psychologist Leon Mann has demonstrated that being in a crowd can facilitate cruel behavior. He studied 15 years of newspaper stories reporting suicide attempts in which someone was threatening to jump from a building, bridge or other great height. In ten of the 21 instances that included crowds at the scene some in the crowd encouraged the suicidal person to jump. In three of the instances there was jeering when rescuers prevented the suicide. Mann posited the crowd's distance from the potential jumper enabled their jeering and baiting to be heard but made their faces impossible to identify, thus making the onlookers feel anonymous (Mann, 1981).

VI. How Should Conflicting Moral Obligations Be Managed?

Two roads diverged in a yellow wood,
And sorry I could not travel both
And be one traveler, long I stood

Robert Frost, "The Road Not Taken"

We had a very difficult situation and we made a difficult call at the end. We live in the real world, we make real decisions. People and kids can climb over barriers. We work hard to make sure this zoo is safe. People can climb over barriers, that's what happened" (Park, Grinberg, and Ap, 2016).

These are the words of Thane Maynard, Director of the Cincinnati Zoo. On May 28, 2016 a three-year-old boy managed to find his way into the zoo's gorilla enclosure where he encountered Harambe, a 450 pound male lowland gorilla. With the gorilla showing signs of agitation and dragging the child around the enclosure there was virtually no time to make a difficult decision. The zoo director had an obligation to rescue the child and an obligation to prevent harm to the gorilla. Almost immediately it was obvious he could not do both. Harambe was killed by a single shot from a rifle. Whenever one moral obligation conflicts with another decision-making has the status of a dilemma.

In a New Testament narrative Jesus is asked if the Jewish people should pay taxes to the Roman Empire. The question was intended as a conundrum in order to discredit Jesus by befuddling him. The Jewish people recognized God as their only king, thereby rejecting Caesar as their ruler. If Jesus advocated nonpayment of taxes, he would have been branded a traitor to Rome. If he encouraged payment of taxes, he would have lost favor in the Jewish community. His answer adequately addressed what seemed to be conflicting obligations:

> But Jesus, knowing their evil intent, said, "You hypocrites, why are you trying to trap me?" Show me the coin used for paying the tax." They brought him a denarius, and he asked them, "Whose portrait is this? And whose inscription?" "Caesar's," they replied. Then he said, "Give to Caesar's what is Caesar's, and to God what is God's" (Matthew 22:18-21).

According to Jesus, the obligations actually were not in conflict. Since Rome's requirement was monetary, paying taxes to Caesar would take nothing away from God. And since God's requirement is obedience to the Ten Commandments and 603 other mitzvah (laws) found in the Hebrew Bible, adherence to God's law would take nothing away from Caesar. In this instance there only seemed to be a conflict.

However, such is not always the case. Sir Thomas More, Chancellor to King Henry VIII, had to choose between loyalty to his King and obedience to his Pope, Clement VII. When the King determined he would divorce Catherine of Aragon and marry Anne Boleyn, Sir Thomas refused to support Henry's decision and agreed with the Pope's refusal to annul the marriage. This led to More's trial and conviction for treason and execution by decapitation in 1535.

Another instance of a church and state conflict, albeit with less dire consequences, is that of Eric Liddell. An almost certain track and field gold medalist for England in the 1924 Olympic Games, Liddell refused to run on the Sabbath, thereby sacrificing the opportunity for the medal. He resisted the urging of his future king, the Prince of Wales, who tried to convince Liddell he had a patriotic obligation to participate. Liddell remained steadfast in his conviction and did not compete in the 100 meter sprint he was almost certain to win.

The practice of medicine also provides occasions for conflicting obligations. A well-known instance is Dr. Jack Kevorkian's administration of a lethal cocktail (combination of medications) to Thomas Youk, who was suffering from Lou Gehrig's disease and requested physician-assisted suicide. The procedure was performed in Michigan, where physician-assisted suicide was and remains illegal. Kevorkian was convicted of second degree murder and sentenced to ten to 15 years imprisonment. He served eight years, was paroled in 2007, and died in 2011 at the age of 83. As a physician, Kevorkian was confronted with oppositional obligations. When he graduated from the University of Michigan Medical School in 1952 he affirmed the Hippocratic Oath which conferred upon him the obligations to alleviate patient suffering and refrain from administering lethal medications to a patient. In the case of Thomas Youk, Kevorkian opted for euthanasia, convinced it was the only means for alleviating the patient's suffering.

Obviously, Kevorkian believed there are cases in which the compassionate thing to do is physician-assisted suicide. This would constitute "the most loving act" principle advocated by Fletcher (Chapter IV). Youk had requested this action and provided written and video recorded informed consent, demonstrating the exercise of free will advocated by de Beauvoir (Chapter IV). Further, by addressing Youk as a suffering human being in need of pain relief, Kevorkian placed the patient above the law. Hence, it could be argued Kevorkian acted in a manner consistent with Kant's categorical imperatives of universality, human dignity, and reciprocity (Chapter IV). A similar situation, referred to in chapter I, confronted Dr. Max Scur when he administered a lethal dose of morphine to Sigmund Freud, who had asked Schur to promise, "when the time comes, you won't let them torment me unnecessarily" (Gay, 1989, pp. 642-643). Like Kevorkian, Schur placed alleviation of his patient's pain above the Hippocratic prohibition of lethal medications.

Another striking occurrence of conflicting obligations confronted helicopter pilot Hugh Thompson at My Lai, the Vietnam War incident referred to in chapter IV. First, disbelieving what he saw from a low hover over the My Lai hamlet and then appalled by the wanton, indefensible slaughter he was witnessing, Major Thompson decided to act to stop the killing. Assigned to protect soldiers on the ground, he landed his helicopter and ordered his machine gunners to turn their weapons on the American troops if they continued killing the helpless Vietnamese. Thompson is hailed as a hero in sociologist Samuel Oliner's book, *Do Unto Others: Extraordinary Acts of Ordinary People*. There Oliner writes, "The courage of this helicopter pilot and his rescue of innocent Vietnamese civilians at My Lai is a particularly compelling example of an unusual kind of military heroism" (2007, p. 117). Thompson weighed and considered his mission to protect soldiers on the ground against his moral obligation to protect defenseless people and acted in favor of the latter.

Principles are necessary for prioritizing conflicting obligations. Without guidelines, moral decision-making is left to the feelings of the decision-makers. However agreeable or compassionate might be the actions of More, Liddell, Kevorkian, Schur, and Thompson, it would be unwise and unjust to approve of a moral action merely because it emanates from the sentiments of the actor. Recall that Lieutenant William Calley participated in the killings at My Lai and did so feeling that he was doing the right thing. (He later expressed regret for following the order he claimed he was given to "waste" My Lai.)

A prerequisite for prioritizing conflicting obligations is establishing the source of the obligations. Without considering the origins of conflicting duties it would be impossible to prioritize them. For Sir Thomas More and Eric Liddell it was a matter of subordinating an earthly obligation to a heavenly responsibility. This principle was declared by the Apostle Peter when he and the other apostles appeared before the Jewish ruling council.

> Having brought in the apostles, they made them appear before the Sanhedrin to be questioned by the high priest. "We gave you strict orders not to teach in this name (Jesus)," he said. "Yet you have filled Jerusalem with your teaching and are determined to make us guilty of this man's blood." Peter and the other apostles replied: "We must obey God rather than men!" (Acts 5:27-29).

For Drs. Kevorkian and Schur it was a matter of preferring the dying wish of a suffering human being over an oath. For Major Thompson it was a matter of saving lives rather than following orders that had become irrelevant.

Navy SEAL Chris Kyle, the most lethal sniper in American military history, reflected on his duty with these words, "Every person I killed I strongly believe that they were bad. When I do go face God there is going to be lots of things I will have to account for, but killing any of those people is not one of them" (2015). Prioritizing obligations, conflicting as well as nonconflicting, requires obedience to conscience and a willingness to take responsibility.

Thought Exercise: "The Confession"

Father Garbriel hears the confession of a man whose voice the priest recognizes. He is certain the confessing man is X. The confession is shocking and disturbing. X confesses to having sexually abused his eight-year-old niece, the daughter of his sister. Father Gabriel appeals to the man to tell his sister what he's done and have her arrange counseling for her daughter. Further, the priest advises X to end all contact with his niece and seek out counseling for himself without disclosing anything specific that would require the counselor to act as a mandated reporter. (As a priest, Father Gabriel is not a mandated reporter and is required to maintain "priest - penitent confidentiality.")

Questions for Consideration

1. In your opinion, does Father Gabriel have a moral obligation beyond the counsel he has given X?

2. Is it justifiable to exempt the clergy from being "mandated reporters" while teachers, physicians, and mental health professionals are not exempt? (Note: Attorneys are not legally required to report suspected or known child abuse, but in some jurisdictions they are permitted to use their discretion.)

3. In a criminal proceeding, a spouse cannot be compelled to testify against a spouse. This includes cases of child abuse.

What is the reason for this feature of the law? In your opinion, is it a necessary and important feature?

Thought Experiment: Your Best Friend's Partner

One evening you receive a text from your best friend's partner with whom your best friend has been in a relationship for about a year. The partner asks to meet for a conversation to discuss something "very important." You agree to meet at a nearby coffee shop.

There you are told by the partner, "I've been wanting to tell you this for a long time: I'm very attracted to you. I think about you all the time and I just have to know if there's any possibility that we could 'get together' in any way you might want to 'get together.'"

This offer is complicated by your attraction to this person who has just declared an interest in you.

<u>Questions for Consideration</u>

1. How are you going to respond to this opportunity?

2. What principle or principles will guide your decision-making?

VII. Does the End Justify the Means?

For what shall it profit a man, if he shall gain the whole world, and lose his own soul?

- Jesus, Mark 8:36 (King James Version)

The end may justify the means as long as there is something that justifies the end.

- Leon Trotsky

Nothing justifies the deaths of innocent people.

- Albert Camus

"The end justifies the means" is a principle associated with Niccolo Machiavelli, author of *The Prince*, a political treatise published in 1515. This principle is often misunderstood as proposing any action, regardless of its apparent immorality, is justified if it effects the desired outcome. This misunderstanding results from overreaching Machiavelli's intention. He was not addressing ethics in general but referring to any action a ruler might take to stabilize the government, retain power or coerce resistant subjects. Machiavelli was not advocating unbridled individual activity for personal gain or self-gratification.

Given this limited scope, the principle nevertheless remains ambiguous in its application. President Truman's decision to deploy the atomic bomb, referred to in chapter IV, persists as controversial even though it stabilized the government of the United States. The end justifies the means is an ethical concept lacking criteria for determining what constitutes a necessary end. Because of this deficit it cannot be employed alone for moral decision-making. Value theory provides what this principle lacks. Value theory is the subcategory of philosophy that addresses the question: *What factors make one thing worth more than another?* Because it is a significant subdivision of philosophy, this chapter is not the place for a concentrated study of the guidelines it provides. Instead, the following two examples clarify the necessity of value theory for moral decision-making.

The proliferation of Canada geese, described in Chapter III, provided the occasion for an intense debate among the citizens of Winchester, Massachusetts - a debate that occurred in spite of their agreement on the seriousness of the problem. The debate derived from their disagreement on whether the problem was sufficiently severe to necessitate killing the geese. Implicit in their debate was the question: Which is more important, preservation of annoying wildlife or maintenance of a pristine town? Clearly, this situation involved competing interests with the best interest of the residents in conflict with that of the geese. How could the cleanliness and pleasantness of the town be weighed against the lives of the geese? Would the end - a clean town, justify the means - killing the geese?

On January 19, 1987 a man left Massachusetts General Hospital where he was being treated for a tropical parasite he had contracted 16 years earlier. He drove to Boston Harbor, parked his car, and committed suicide by drowning. The man was the renowned Harvard psychology professor Lawrence Kohlberg, whose research on moral development is described in virtually every introductory and developmental psychology textbook published in the last 25 years. Was Dr. Kohlberg's final act morally wrong? Does it matter that he had suffered both physical pain and depression since 1971 because of his illness? Does it matter that the prognosis was the worst is yet to come? Did the end - cessation of his pain, justify the means – his suicide?

"Hard cases make bad law" is a maxim among jurists (Holdsworth, 1926, IX, p. 423). The situations of President Truman, the citizens of Winchester, and Professor Kohlberg qualify as hard cases. The question in moral decision-making is not: *Does the end ever justify the means?* Rather, the question is: *What are the criteria for determining when an end's worthiness justifies any and every means?* Regarding this question, there are at least two possible answers: (1) When it is a matter of life and death. (2) When the damage to be inflicted by the means is minuscule compared to the benefit it will provide.

When it is a matter of life and death?

This guideline is consistent with Immanuel Kant's categorical imperative that one person should never use another person as a means to an end (Chapter IV). This principle denounces slavery, since it makes one person, the slave, a means to the end of financial gain for another person, the slave owner. There is something else to be derived from this principle: if a human life would be saved by an act that is usually considered immoral then the act would not be immoral. An instance of this is exceeding the speed limit to transport a person with a life-threatening injury to the emergency room. According to Kant's principle, the end (saving a life) trumps the means (breaking the law).

When the damage inflicted by the means is minuscule compared to the benefit it provides.

The example used in the previous section could also be used in this section. The damage inflicted by exceeding the speed limit is minuscule compared to the benefit of saving a life. A mundane life event is telling a lie when the truth would hurt someone for no apparent reason. The following story serves as an illustration:

The pastor always moved to the back of the sanctuary when the congregation was singing the closing hymn. From there he would give the benediction and dismiss his flock. He would then place himself just inside the front door so he could individually greet the congregants as they exited the church. The pastor enjoyed this concluding ritual and his parishioners never seemed to mind the five or so minutes it required.

An elderly widow was one of the last to receive the pastor's wish for a "good Sabbath." She was the kind of woman to be found in every church, regardless of denomination, and deferentially referred to as "Sister." The pastor was unable to cup her frail and withered hands gently in both of his because she was carrying a pie. Reminiscent of a child presenting a straight-A report card to a parent, Sister could barely contain her excitement as she placed it his hands. In a frail voice she managed, "Pastor, I hope you and your family enjoy this pie."

The pastor knew for this woman baking a pie was a herculean labor. He responded, "Thank you, Sister. This will be our dessert today. Have a blessed Sabbath."

That afternoon, after dinner, the pie's tin foil covering was removed with the unveiling came a delightful aroma that was immediately recognized as rhubarb. A slice was cut for each family member as the Pastor informed them their dessert was a gift from Sister. As they had been taught, the children waited until everyone at the table had been served. With the coordination of synchronized swimmers, the family placed the first forkful of pie in their mouths. Too refined to spit out the unpalatable, the pastor and his family swallowed their first—and last—taste of the pie.

Stunned silence was followed as each looked to the other for confirmation that in a world with millions of pies they had just sampled the most inedible. The phrase, "It goes without saying" was made for moments like this.

The pastor's wife broke the silence, "What are you going to tell Sister?" The wastebasket was circulated to receive uneaten pieces of the pie as well as the half that remained in the pie tin.

That week the pastor spent as much time contemplating the answer to his wife's question as he spent preparing his sermon. What is one to do with the truth when it would hurt someone and serve no good purpose? To tell Sister her pie was delicious would spare her feelings but encourage her to inflict another pie on his family and unsuspecting others. He felt the weight of simultaneous obligations to tell the truth and protect an elderly woman's feelings. He wrestled with the conflicting obligations aware that his children would be watching.

The next Sunday morning, the pastor's thoughts alternated between his sermon and the impending encounter with Sister. He hadn't decided what he was going to say to her when she asked, "Did you and your family enjoy the pie?"

The sermon was delivered, closing hymn sung, and benediction given. The congregants, including Sister, formed a queue for the pastoral greeting. Unencumbered by a pie, she extended her hand to the Pastor and asked, "Did you and your family enjoy the rhubarb pie?"

With neither rehearsal nor hesitation he responded, "Let me tell you something Sister, a pie like that doesn't last long around our house!"

No apparent damage was done by the Pastor's double entendre and considerable pain would have resulted if the Pastor had unambiguously described the family's reaction to the pie. If the end justifies the means when the damage inflicted by the means is minuscule compared to the benefit of the end then the Pastor's ambiguity is morally justifiable.

This is not to say a person's feelings should always be spared at the expense of the truth. In Amy Chua's *Battle Hymn of the Tiger Mother* she recounts refusing a birthday card from her 4-year-old daughter, Lulu.

> Lulu handed me her "surprise," which turned out to be a card. More accurately, it was a piece of paper folded crudely in half, with a big happy face on the front. Inside, "Happy Birthday, Mommy! Love, Lulu" was scrawled in crayon above another happy face. The card couldn't have taken Lulu more than twenty seconds to make.
>
> I gave the card back to Lulu. "I don't want this," I said. "I want a better one – one that you've put some thought and effort into. I have a special box where I keep all my cards from you and Sophia (Lulu's sister), and this one can't go in there."
>
> I grabbed the card again and flipped it over. I pulled out a pen from my purse and scrawled "Happy Birthday Lulu Whoopee!" I added a big sour face. "What if I gave you this for your birthday, Lulu - would you like that?" (2011, p. 103).

Anecdotes like this account for the controversy surrounding Amy Chua's book and widespread criticism of her parenting. She believes, "it's too idealistic to expect children to do the right things on their own. Also, if you force them to do what you want, you don't have to be mad at them" (p. 104). For Amy Chua, but not for everybody, the end of sparing Lulu's feelings was not sufficient to justify withholding from her the truth that she had produced something well below her best effort. Amy Chua's determination to nurture her children to strive for excellence justified her rejection of a mediocre birthday card.

The determination of when an end is justified by its means is no simple matter. Some of Winchester's citizens argued that an unpolluted town would justify killing the geese while others disagreed. Some, but not everyone, would argue the cessation of Professor Kohlberg's unremitting pain justified his suicide. The atomic bombs were dropped on Hiroshima and Nagasaki 75 years ago, yet the controversy over the moral rightness of President Truman's decision continues in the present.

Concerning issues like lying and abortion it seems impossible to advocate an extreme position. Although Sam Harris believes lying is morally wrong, he admits there are some situations in which a lie is the lesser of two evils:

> If there are Nazis at the door, and you've got Anne Frank in the attic, then I view lying the way most people do – as a necessary act of self-defense or the defense of others. I consider lying to be on a continuum of violence, where it's generally the least

violent thing you can do to someone who's no longer behaving rationally (2020, p. 264)

Similarly, even among those who oppose abortions are those who allow for an abortion that would save the life of a pregnant woman.

Historian Steven Mintz writes of "the end" as a *destination* and "the means" as a *journey*:

> The reason the means are important, maybe more important than the ends, is how we get to our goal is just as important as getting there. In other words, destiny tells us what we are to the world, but journey tells who we are; it's the journey that unlocks our potential and establishes who we are as a person and what motivates us towards action (2018).

VIII. Is Justice Always Moral?

Woe to you, scribes and Pharisees, hypocrites! For you tithe mint and dill and cummin, and have neglected the weightier provisions of the law: justice and mercy and faithfulness; but these are the things you should have done without neglecting the others. You blind guides, who strain out a gnat and swallow a camel.

-Jesus, (Matthew 23:23,24)

The Imperfect Perfect Game

On June 2, 2010, Armando Gallaraga, a pitcher for the Detroit Tigers, retired twenty-six consecutive Cleveland Indians. He appeared to have achieved the so-called perfect game in which no batter reaches base when the twenty-seventh Indian batter hit a routine ground ball fielded by the Tigers' first baseman and tossed to Gallaraga covering first base for the final out. The celebration of this rare event turned to protest when first base umpire Jim Joyce made an obvious error and called the runner safe, depriving Gallaraga of what would have been the twenty-third perfect game in major league baseball's 135 year history.

At this time baseball had no provision for video tape reviews and reversals of incorrect calls by umpires. When Joyce saw the replay after the game he admitted his error. The only person with the authority to overrule Joyce's call was the Commissioner of Major League Baseball, Bud Selig. He refused to do so, reasoning it would be the first time a Commissioner overturned an umpire's judgment call and would establish an unwise precedent. Selig's decision was consistent with a principle of jurisprudence: *the law is concerned with neither right nor wrong – only precedent.* Was justice served by the Commissioner's decision? His critics argue that precedent should be set aside when it perpetuates an obvious injustice. Selig's supporters posit that without strict adherence to precedent there is no reliable system for dispensing justice.

The Firing of Melissa Nelson

Melissa Nelson worked as a dental assistant for ten years and thought she would make it her lifelong career. But that came to a sudden end in 2010 when her boss fired her for being too attractive. Fort Dodge, Iowa dentist James Knight said he fired Nelson to save his marriage. Justice Edward Mansfield wrote that such firings are not unlawful discrimination because they are motivated by feelings and emotions, not gender. Nelson and her attorney, Page Fielder, disputed the ruling and hope to have it overturned. Fielder filed a petition this week requesting a hearing.

"The only reason he was attracted to her at all was because she is a woman," Fielder said. "The fact that it came from his feelings is not inconsistent with the fact that she's a woman. Since they admitted it, it's perplexing to me why it was dismissed."

Brad Dacus, President of the Pacific Justice Institute, said that anyone who understands the male psyche knows that it would have been difficult for the dentist to turn off his feelings for Nelson. "Men and women think differently," said Dacus.

Terry O'Neil, President of the National Organization for Women," called the firing, "Harassment in its classic form" (*Huffington Post*, 2013).

There was nothing illegal about the firing of Melissa Nelson, but this alone doesn't make her firing morally right. As the Rev. Dr. Martin Luther King, Jr. pointed out, "We must never forget that everything Hitler did was legal" (1997).

Universal and Particular Justice

Aristotle's philosophy of justice, presented in the *Nicomachean Ethics,* makes a distinction between *universal justice* – that which is absolutely morally right, and *particular justice* – that which is right relative to a specific situation. In a perfect society moral absolutes could determine justice in every situation. However, specific situations sometimes require a deviation from moral absolutes if justice is to be served. In the previous chapter it is argued although honesty is respected as a virtue, there are times when withholding the truth or even lying might serve a greater good. If telling a lie would save a life it would be justifiable as a contribution to particular justice. Returning to the Baseball Commissioner's decision, his strict adherence to precedent is an instantiation of *universal justice.* Had he suspended the rule and overturned the umpire's call it would have been an instantiation of *particular justice.*

Justice, one of the Four Cardinal Virtues, is sufficiently complicated to warrant three subcategories: *distributive, compensatory,* and *retributive.* In this chapter each is addressed separately.

Distributive Justice

Distributive justice is concerned with an equitable share of benefits and burdens. *Equal* and *equitable* are not synonyms. The former means "same in amount;" the latter means "proper and fair." Consider four people who receive the bill for the lunch they have enjoyed together. If they decide to pay *equally* they will simply add a tip to the amount and divide by four. But what if one of them enjoyed two glasses of wine at $12 each while the other three were content to drink water? If they determine the amount each will contribute according to the cost of each meal and beverage, they will be contributing *equitably.*

A *Los Angeles Times* news story provides a remarkable example of an unusual distribution of burden.

Father 30 Times Over Seeks Break in Child Support

Desmond Hatchett, 33, is something of a local celebrity in Knoxville, Tenn. In 2009, in a t.v. interview, he proclaimed, "I'm done!" - that he wouldn't father more children.

Now, with 30 children by 11 women, he wants a break on child-support payments. The youngest is a toddler; the oldest is 14. Hatchett has a minimum wage job, and he struggles to make ends meet. He's required to turn over 50 percent of his wages for child support – the maximum under law (*Huffington Post*, 2012).

At the time of the story Hatchett was in prison for failure to pay child support. The burden of supporting the children he's fathered has fallen upon their mothers, charity, and public assistance.

A letter to the editor from a Syracuse, New York newspaper addresses the question: "Who decides what makes a fair share?"

To the editor:

The next time I hear anyone say, "The rich should pay their fair share," my hair is going to hurt. Surely, this is a vacuous statement. (Please refrain from saying, "Don't call me Shirley.") Who are "the rich" and how is this determined? What constitutes a "fair share" and who decides?

The Marxist dictum, "From each according to his ability, to each according to his needs" disregards human nature by naively assuming people maximally produce while minimally benefitting. Ayn Rand produced two novels totaling 1,500 pages conveying the philosophy the rich have no philanthropic obligation to the poor. Similarly, Aesop implied that industrious ants are not morally required to subsidize indolent grasshoppers.

Like jurors betwixt dueling experts in a civil case, how are we to determine liability and what it should be? I suggest that before declaring how other people's wealth should be distributed, a bit of self-examination is in order. The Parable of the Good Samaritan (Luke 10:30-37) was told by Jesus in response to the question: "Who is my neighbor?" I submit here we have a starting point for answering the questions, "Who are the rich?" and, "What is their fair share?"

The next time you encounter a panhandler, consider how you are responding and, if you give, how much. Feeling rich? Giving a fair share? These questions are not intended to provoke guilt, but to clarify what you *really* believe. Then consider this thought from Herman Hesse: "The hardest road is the one that leads a man to himself" (*The Post Standard*, 11/18/11)

Concerning the fair distribution of benefit, there is no shortage of anecdotes describing the sense of entitlement felt by family members and friends of some lottery winners (Stossel, 1998). Requesters often express anger, indignation, or both if they are denied a gift or loan. Bob Harrell, a Texas Lotto winner, committed suicide two years after winning $31 million (McVicker, 2000). William Post was on food stamps a year after winning $16.2 million in the Pennsylvania Lottery (Sullivan, 2006). Friends and family insisting on a share of the winnings contributed to the sad ending of both stories.

Compensatory Justice

Political philosopher John Rawls determined, "Procedural justice does not guarantee justice of outcome" (1971, II, 14). Ethics philosopher John Boatright agrees and writes,

> Trial by jury is not a perfect procedure, but any alternative is worse. So unless we are willing to accept the verdicts of juries – even when the outcome is the conviction of an innocent person or the exoneration of a guilty one – the result is likely to be even more unjust outcomes (1993, p. 94).

Roy Brown is well aware of the criminal justice system's imperfection. In 2009 he received $2.6 million from the State of New York as compensation for 15 years imprisonment for a murder he did not commit. Was he fairly compensated?

Jonathan Harr's bestseller, *A Civil Action,* chronicles the lawsuit and settlement of a case of irresponsible waste disposal in Woburn, Massachusetts (1996). Eight cases of leukemia were connected to drinking water contaminated by chemical dumping. The $8 million settlement resulted in $375,000 for each family. How much money is just compensation for a child who contracted cancer in this way?

Was tennis player Roger Federer fairly compensated in 2019 when he earned $106 million? He outearned singer Elton John and writer James Patterson, both of whom earned $80 million in 2020. Compare these staggering amounts to $61,730, the national average annual salary of public school teachers, and ponder whether teachers are adequately compensated (National Center for Education Statistics, 2020).

H.R. 40

H.R. 240 is legislation pending in the United States House of Representatives. It's currently being considered by the Committee to Study and Develop Reparations Proposals for the African-American Act. The committee's task is to study the continuing effects of slavery and, possibly, recommend means of rectifying the harm done to the descendants of slaves. The bill is labeled H.R. 40 in reference to an unfulfilled promise made by the government in 1866 to provide "40 acres and a mule" to emancipated slaves as compensation for unpaid labor. Both advocates and opponents of H.R. 40 are to be found not only in Congress but in the country at large.

If H.R. 40 passes a commission will consider arguments for and against reparations. One argument of the opposition is the judicial system already has an available remedy for those harmed by slavery. This remedy is a civil action in which the defendant's liability is considered and, if established, damages are awarded to the plaintiff. Opponents to H.R. 40 further argue that people living 500 years after the first slaves were brought to America are not responsible for slavery or its consequences. Hence, there can be no defendants. Moreover, descendants of slaves living today cannot claim damages without specifying the harm done to them in terms of financial or other losses. Without measurable damages there can be no victims. Another oppositional argument is the statute of limitations has expired because the clock to initiate a civil action starts ticking from the date of the inflicted harm or discovery of the harm, but no more than two years with few exceptions. (None of which applies to reparations.)

The opposition's arguments can be summarized by a moral principle favored by some philosophers: *the rule of common sense.* Common sense morality is the moral principles by which people actually live rather than the esoteric theories provided by philosophers. H.R. 40's opponents submit common sense dictates it is illogical and immoral to hold people responsible for something done at least 150 years before they were born.

Those favoring reparations argue damages can be quantified and offer a daunting figure concerning them. One figure derives from the aforementioned "40 acres and a mule" calculating an acre of land valued at $10 in 1865 times 40 acres equals $400 times four million (the number of slaves in the United States in 1865) for a total of $1.6 billion. Accounting for interest and inflation, $1.6 billion in 1865 adjusts to $2.6 trillion dollars in 2019. This would mean approximately $87,000 to be given to each of the estimated 30 million slave descendants currently living in the United States. (Note: The mule was not a part of this calculation.)

Proponents of H.R. 40 also cite the precedent of 800,000 Japanese Americans who were sent to internment camps during World War II and each given $20,000. Another precedent is the 1953 reparations agreement between West Germany and Israel in which West Germany compensated displaced Jewish people for losses of property and livelihood resulting from Nazi persecution.

People on both sides of this issue could quote from renowned thinkers. Opponents could cite Jean-Paul Sartre: "Man is nothing else than his plan; he exists only to the extent that he fulfills himself; he is therefore nothing else than the ensemble of his acts" (1957, p. 32). Proponents could direct the attention of Congress to the words of Jesus: "From everyone who has been given much, much will be demanded; and from the one who has been entrusted with much, much more will be asked" (Luke 12:48).

Retributive Justice

"Let the punishment fit the crime" is a familiar aphorism to lawyers and laypersons alike. The Eighth Amendment to the *United States Constitution* prohibits "cruel and inhumane punishment" for violations of the law. *Retributive justice* is concerned with the question: What constitutes a fair punishment for a given crime?

The opening scene of the movie *The Godfather* is a distraught father meeting with Don Corleone, the Godfather. The man's daughter was savagely beaten by two men who attempted to rape her. She absorbed a horrific beating fending off the rape. The father's anguish was exacerbated when the two assailants received only a suspended sentence for their assault. He asks Don Corleone to have the young men killed. The Godfather refused, saying, "That's not justice; your daughter is alive." He did agree, however, to arrange to have the young woman's beating replicated. The two young men received injury for injury the same beating they administered to the man's daughter. This is talion law, characterized by the biblical instruction, "An eye for an eye ..." (Exodus 1:24).

An April, 2013 news story reported the sentencing of a man in Saudi Arabia to medical paralyzation. Ali Al-Khawahir, age 24, was found guilty of stabbing a man in the back, paralyzing him. The court ruled that Al-Khawahir must pay his victim approximately $250,000 or Al-Khawahir will have his spinal cord surgically cut to induce paralysis. Ann Harrison of Amnesty International expressed indignation at this instance of eye-for-eye justice: "That such a punishment might be implemented is utterly shocking, even in a context where flogging is frequently imposed as a punishment for some offenses, as happens in Saudi Arabia" (Grenoble, 2013).

No issue of retributive justice has been more controversial than capital punishment. Currently, there are 2,000 prisoners awaiting execution in the United States in the 30 states that allow for the death penalty. In 12 of these states there have been no executions in the last ten years. In 2020 there were 17 executions in the United States, 16 by lethal injection and one by electrocution.

A letter written in 1912 provides a remarkable response to fatal punishment. It was written by the father of Edgar Farrar, Jr., who had been killed in a burglary by Rene Canton. Eight days before Canton's execution the governor of Louisiana received a letter from the father of the man killed by Canton:

His Excellency, Luther E. Hall,
Governor of Louisiana
Baton Rouge, LA.

Dear Sir:

On this day of Thanksgiving, the thoughts of all my household were turned to the chair made empty by the crime of the poor wretch, the date of whose execution you have fixed. This matter has been in our minds for some time, and after mature deliberation, all of us, father, mother, sisters, brothers and widow of my son, have concluded to ask you to reprieve Rene Canton, and to send his case before the Board of Pardons for their consideration as to whether his sentence should not be commuted to imprisonment for life. We feel that this young brute is the product of our system of society, for which all of us, particularly persons of our position, are to some extend responsible. His father and mother are honest, hardworking people. With them the struggle for existence was too bitter and exacting to permit them to devote the time and personal care necessary to develop the good and repress the evil in their son, who thus grew up amid the malign influences that surround the children of the poor in a large city. We believe that he shot my son as instinctively as a snake would strike one who crossed his path; and while his act was murder in law and fact, yet it lacked the forethought and deliberation which make a crime of this sort unpardonable. This man is now in no condition to be sent into the next world. We hope and pray that time and reflection will bring repentance and that his soul may be saved.

Your obedient servant,

Edgar Howard Farrar

(Farrar, 1997, p. 402)

Civil Disobedience

Civil disobedience is the refusal to obey certain laws, sometimes, but not necessarily, employing violence. It's a term associated with the philosopher Henry David Thoreau. In his essay *Civil Disobedience* he expresses his opposition to the Mexican-American War and the United States' allowance of slavery:

> How does it become a man to behave toward the American government today? I answer, that he cannot without disgrace be associated with it. I cannot for an instant recognize that political organization as *my* government which is the *slave's* government also (2014, p. 6).

Chapter I includes the Rev. Dr. Martin Luther King, Jr.'s rationale for disobeying unjust laws. In his Letter from Birmingham Jail he explains how to distinguish between just and unjust laws. King was influenced by Thoreau, having read *Civil Disobedience* as a student:

> Fascinated by the idea of refusing to cooperate with an evil system, I was so deeply moved that I reread the work several times. I became convinced that noncooperation with evil is as much a moral obligation as is cooperation with good (2001, p. 14).

IX. Is Lying Always Morally Wrong?

That lying is a necessity of life is itself a part of the problematic character of existence.

- Friedrich Nietzsche

Truthfulness in statements is the formal duty of an individual to everyone, however great may be the disadvantage according to himself or to another.

- Immanuel Kant

The final scene in *The Godfather I* portrays Michael Corleone lying to his wife, Kay, after she asked him if he killed their brother-in-law, Carlo. Unable to dissuade her questioning by reminding her of their understanding that she would never ask about his business affairs, he relents and lies to her with a one-word denial: "No." The scene and movie end with a greatly relieved Kay embracing Michael, not doubting that she has heard the truth and unaware that the stage has been set for *The Godfather II*.

This chapter addresses the behavior of lying. Stated as a question, this chapter asks: *Is it always morally wrong to lie or is lying something we all must inevitably do in order to effectively manage life?* Before proceeding, a definition of *lie* is in order. As a noun, a lie is "a false statement or piece of information deliberately presented as a falsehood." As a verb, lying is "to present information with the intention of deceiving; to convey a false image or impression" (*American Heritage Dictionary*, 1973, p. 754).

Noteworthy is that lying is *not* one of the seven deadly sins (pride, envy, anger, sloth, avarice, gluttony, and lust). Neither is lying's antithesis, truth-telling, listed among the four cardinal virtues (temperance, fortitude, justice, and prudence). Still, it could be argued that telling the truth often requires courage (fortitude), fairness (justice), and wisdom (prudence). It cannot be taken lightly that our parents instructed us to be unswervingly honest with injunctions like, "No matter what you've done, always tell us the truth." Few, if any of us, were instructed to tell the truth selectively or lie judiciously.

Tolerable Lies

There is almost unanimous agreement among philosophers that "the complicated nature of human affairs" requires sporadic, intentional deception (Martin, 1995, p. 70). Immanuel Kant is a conspicuous exception. "Unlike most of his followers, he believed there is an *absolute* (exceptionless) duty never to lie" (p. 64). An oft employed hypothetical scenario supporting the majority view is the hiding of Jews in Nazi era Germany. It's absurd to think a rescuer harboring Jews would answer honestly if asked by a Gestapo officer, "Are you hiding Jews?" Parents routinely insist their children misrepresent the truth when they are told to express appreciation for a gift they neither want nor like. In a magazine essay, "Liar, Liar, Parents on Fire," Katherine Deveny admits to lying to her daughter:

> When my daughter asked me why it was embarrassing that former New York governor Eliot Spitzer was involved with a cowgirl ring, I didn't hesitate. "Bad lariat tricks," I explained. She looked a little confused, but I let it drop. I know that I'm not supposed to lie to my kid, but I didn't feel like explaining prostitution to a 7-year old. But it is hardly the first whopper I've told my child, and it got me thinking about how I really feel about honesty as a policy (*Newsweek,* 04/07/08).

After considering the matter, Deveny concluded,

> I'm going to try to stop lying to my daughter because I want her to trust me, and because I don't want her to learn that lying is an effective strategy for dealing with the adult world. Even if that's the sad truth (04/07/08).

Is it a sad truth that lying is a necessary evil? Further, are there situations in which lying might be considered a noble act even if the term *honorable lies* has an oxymoronic tone? Another sad truth is conflicts between virtues occur. Lawrence Kohlberg's *moral stages theory* includes *stage four* (rules and laws should be obeyed) and *stage five* (sometimes rules and laws must be suspended to serve a greater good) (1984). Lying or in some other way deceiving the Gestapo in its search for

Jews would be a stage five instantiation as well as an honorable lie. Similarly, when the late Senator John McCain was a prisoner of war, he gave his interrogators the names of the Green Bay Packers' offensive line when asked for the names of the men in his squadron.

Lying to save people from a concentration camp, withhold confusing information from a child, and shield comrades have something in common. In each of these instances the lie is for the benefit of someone other than the liar. If there is such a thing as honorable lying, it is done in the service of others. Dr. Benjamin Carson, a noted pediatric neurosurgeon, recounts a deception from which he and his brother benefitted.

> My mother was a domestic. Through her work, she observed that successful people spent a lot more time reading than they did watching television. She announced that my brother and I had to read two books each (every week) and submit to her written book reports. She would mark them up with check marks and highlights. Years later we realized her marks were a ruse, My mother was illiterate; she had only received a third grade education (2006, pp. 28-29).

However, this is not to say that *any* lie that provides a benefit to someone other than the liar is noble. The benefit of the deception must be substantial to the one being deceived - a judgment often not easily made. A husband might choose to withhold from his wife that he has committed adultery knowing she would be devastated to learn of his betrayal. However, not knowing of his infidelity mitigates her exercise of free will since she will not have the opportunity to decide if she wants to be married to a man who has been unfaithful. The obvious benefit of nondisclosure for him would be avoidance of considerable discomfort and embarrassment.

It's possible for a lie to serve the interest of the liar, put the recipient at a disadvantage, yet still be tolerable. In football games quarterbacks deceive the defense by faking passes on running plays. In poker, bluffing is a deceptive maneuver by which a player bets heavily on a poor hand or lightly on a good one. It seems odd to refer to these activities as lying since they are understood by the participants as part of the contest. Nevertheless, play-faking and bluffing are strategic deceptions.

An especially interesting type of lie is one the recipient assumes is a lie. Interrogating police officers and cross examining attorneys often assume they are being lied to and account for this in their questioning. While attempts to deceive police officers and juries are not morally right they are often taken for granted.

Lying as a Necessary Evil

Since lying includes all forms of intentional deception, it is appropriate to turn attention to misrepresentations in scientific research. Stanley Milgram's *Obedience and Compliance Experiment*, described in chapter III, is one of psychology's best known investigations (2005). Less well-known, but equally intriguing, is David Rosenhan's "On Being Sane in Insane Places" study (1973). These studies could not have been accomplished without intentional misrepresentations to the subjects. Numerous other studies involve placebos, inert substances that have no medicinal power. Integral to the "placebo effect" is the subjects' belief that they are receiving an actual drug. These deceptions, like play-action fakes in football and bluffing in poker, are rarely thought of as lies. Still, all of them have the common characteristic of withholding the truth. The moral question raised by these practices is one of *cost-benefit analysis* in which the cost of an ethical compromise is weighed against the benefit of some accomplishment.

Figures of speech that combine seemingly contradictory expressions not only add zest to discourse but also imply something about the complexity of life. The oxymoron *necessary evil* communicates that some worthy goal can be reached only by resorting to wrongdoing. (One of the airplanes involved in the atomic bombing of Hiroshima in World War II was named "Necessary Evil.") Driving well above the speed limit and slowing down, but not stopping, at intersections is defensible conduct when rushing an injured child to the emergency room. An honest assessment of some situations would force most people to the conclusion that there are circumstances in which wrongdoing is justifiable.

As previously stated, Immanuel Kant has offered the minority opinion that lying is always morally wrong and should never be employed. "Kant was a duty ethicist, that is, someone who defines right acts as those required by duty. Unlike most of his followers, he believed there is an *absolute - exceptionless* - duty never to lie" (Martin, 1989, p. 57). However, Kant himself would have encountered conflicting ethical imperatives if his duty to always tell the truth would have resulted in someone's death. Truth-telling in such an instance would be contrary to the fundamental duty to respect human life - referred to by Kant as a *categorical imperative*. (Reconsider the example of hiding Jews and being questioned by the Gestapo.) Telling the truth at the expense of someone's life fits the description provided by the wry aphorism, "The operation was a success, but the patient died."

Why Is Lying Unethical?

Perhaps this seems an odd question, given that everybody knows that *honesty is the best policy*. This is precisely what psychologists Martin Seligman and Chris Peterson found in their investigation of universal virtues (2004). Honesty was one of twenty-four *signature strengths*, also referred to as *ubiquitous virtues*, identified in their study of virtues affirmed by all cultures regardless of when or where they exist or have existed.

A biblical condemnation of lying is implied in the Ten Commandments: "You shall not give false testimony against your neighbor" (Deuteronomy 5:20). Divine disapproval of lying is emphatically reinforced in the New Testament where

God strikes dead Ananias and Sapphira for lying (Acts 5: 1-11).

The stereotypical used car salesman who makes car buyers thankful for CARFAX (vehicle history reports) and the "lemon law" (the buyer's right to return a dysfunctional car) has acted unethically when his misrepresentation hinders a prospective buyer's free will decision-making. Unavoidable unknowns make used car buying difficult enough without distortions of the car's history and condition. Kant posited that any mitigation of an individual's autonomy constitutes a violation of the categorical imperative: "Act so that you treat humanity, whether in your own person or in that of another, always as an end and never as a means only" (Martin, p. 58).

When lying serves the interests of the liar - and only the liar - it is an act of selfishness. It is reasonable to speculate if Seligman and Peterson had given themselves to a search for universal vices they would have found lying as one of them. (In spite of its title, Ayn Rand's well-known essay, "The Virtue of Selfishness," does not advocate unbridled self-serving [1961, pp. vii-xii]).

Concluding Thoughts

Lying is akin to speeding in that it is something almost everyone does but admits is wrong. Further, like speeding, it's something most people rationalize but rarely believe anyone else can justify. Lying is recognized as so powerful a temptation that the courts require witnesses to "solemnly swear to tell the truth, the whole truth, and nothing but the truth." (How likely is this thought: "I was fully resolved to lie until I placed my hand on the Bible and promised to tell the truth"?) Regarding "the whole truth," Sissela Bok has written:

> The whole truth is out of reach. But this fact has very little to do with our choices about whether to lie or to speak honestly, about what to say and what to hold back. These choices can be set forth, compared, evaluated, And when they are, even rudimentary distinctions can give guidance (1978, p. 4).

In his classic, *Man's Search for Meaning*, psychiatrist and Holocaust survivor Viktor Frankl describes his concentration camp resolution to tell the truth and so let his fate be determined.

> In Auschwitz I laid down a rule for myself which proved to be a good one and which most of my comrades later followed. I generally answered all kinds of questions truthfully. But I was silent about anything that was not expressly asked for. If I were asked my age, I gave it. If asked about my profession, I said "doctor," but did not elaborate (1959, p. 74).

How many of us, living in far less dire circumstances, would make the same resolution? (The death to survival ratio of those who entered a concentration camp has been calculated at 28:1. Frankl survived, dying in 1997 at age 93.)

Bok's thorough, scholarly treatise, *Lying: Moral Choice in Private and Public Life*, includes the following chapters (1978):

- Is the "Whole Truth" Attainable?
- Weighing the Consequences
- White Lies
- Lies in a Crisis
- Lying to Liars
- Lying to Enemies
- Lies Protecting Peers and Clients
- Lies for the Public Good
- Deceptive Social Science Research
- Lies to the Sick and Dying

This list implies Bok's agreement with John Stuart Mill's observation: "It is not the fault of any creed, but of the complicated nature of human affairs, that rules of conduct cannot be so framed as to require no exceptions" (Martin, 1989, p. 64).

In 1920 anthropologist Frederick Starr and attorney Clarence Darrow debated the question, "Is life worth living?" Darrow's introductory statement included this assessment:

... man does not live by rules. If he did, he would not live. He lives by his emotions, his instincts, his feelings; he lives as he goes along. Man does not make rules of life and then live according to those rules; he lives and then he makes rules of life (MacLaskey and MacLaskey, 1920, p. 15).

X. Is Infidelity Always Wrong?

The married state, with and without the affection suitable to it, is the completest image of heaven and hell we are capable of receiving in this life.

- Richard Steele

In a superbly written, insightful book, *Necessary Losses*, Judith Viorst writes,

> (W)e sometimes hate the married state for domesticating our dreams of romantic love. We bring into our marriage a host of romantic expectations. We may also bring visions of mythic romantic thrills. We should achieve paradise or at least a reasonable facsimile thereof. We will be disappointed (1998, p. 188).

She explains the lure of infidelity often arises out of this disappointment:

> Our friends are less than perfect. We accept their imperfections and pride ourselves on our sense of reality. But when it comes to love we stubbornly cling to our illusions – to conscious and unconscious visions of how things should be (p. 185).

Often, the road to infidelity is paved with rationalization. The climactic line in a popular song from the 1970's is, "It can't be wrong when it feels so right" (Brooks, 1977). And in Robert Waller's classic novel, *The Bridges of Madison County*, Kincaid tries to persuade his adulterous lover, Francesca, to abandon her family and start a new life with him:

> Then they held each other for a long time. And he whispered to her, "I have one thing to say, and one thing only, I'll never say it another time, to anyone, and I ask you to remember it: In a universe of ambiguity, this kind of certainty comes only once, and never again, no matter how many lifetimes you live (1992, p. 117).

In spite of harsh reviews by critics and literary scholars, Waller's novel sold 60 million copies worldwide, making it one of the 20th century's bestselling books. A likely explanation for its international appeal is the ubiquity of devitalized marriages and a longing for romantic passion. Thomas Moore, a former monk and spiritual guide, writes, "Many married people confess to deep ambivalence about being married, and many secretly harbor strong fantasies of divorce and the single life" (1999, p. 208).

What constitutes cheating?

Adultery is voluntary sexual intercourse between a married person and a person who is not his or her spouse. Infidelity is the action or state of being unfaithful to a spouse or partner. "Cheating" is a colloquial term for infidelity. An informal study of 2,700 "singles" from two dating websites reveals some interesting differences between men and women regarding what qualifies as "cheating" (*Huffington Post*, 02/01/2013):

Action	Men	Women
intercourse	95%	100%
passionate kiss	86%	100%
texting online or flirting	56%	80%
"emotional connection" (non-sexual contact)	65%	77%

It might seem odd to ask, "Is infidelity always morally wrong?" It's not challenging to defend faithfulness in a relationship. Religion, philosophy, clinical psychology, and law advocate fidelity. Their contributions are considered in the next subsection. More difficult is making a case for non-exclusivity. Nevertheless, in the last subsection an argument is made for two situations in which non-exclusivity might not be immoral.

Max Malikow

Five Reasons Why Infidelity Is Morally Wrong

1. Infidelity injures the betrayed partner. Anyone who doubts this should see a five minute scene from the movie *Network*, nominated for an Academy Award for Best Picture in 1976. Three of its performers won Academy Awards: Best Actor (Peter Finch), Best Actress (Faye Dunaway), and Best Supporting Actress (Beatrice Straight). What's remarkable about Beatrice Straight's performance is its length: five minutes. The intensity of pain she portrays when her husband tells her of his extramarital affair is palpable.

2. Concerning adultery, it is prohibited by all three of the major monotheistic religions. Christianity forbids it in 16 places in the New Testament. In addition to the seventh of the Ten Commandments, Judaism forbids it in five other passages. Islam teaches against it in chapter 17, verse 32 of the Qur'an: "Do not even go near *zena* (fornication and/or adultery), for it is a very indecent thing and a very evil way." (Islam allows a man to have four wives but he must treat each of his wives equally. Also, he cannot marry another man's wife. Moreover, a man must support each child he fathers and each child is an equal heir to his estate.)

3. Concerning adultery, it is prohibited by law. When a marriage requires a marriage license, as it does in most states, adultery constitutes a violation of a contract. This makes

adultery a civil law violation as well as a ground for divorce. (In some states cohabiting for five years qualifies as a marriage but this determination might require a ruling by a judge.)

4. Infidelity is considered morally wrong when it offends the conscience of the unfaithful partner. (This does not mean it is not morally wrong if the offending party is untroubled by conscience.) Recall the description of the adulterous minister, Reverend Dimmesdale, in chapter II. The renowned psychiatrist and bestselling author Scott Peck confessed to his serial adultery, admitting to it as a moral failure:

> (A)fter a while at least, marriage becomes part of an ordinary earthly existence and in some respects quite humdrum. Lily (Dr. Peck's wife) and I developed different ways of dealing with this dreary reality. Possibly one of hers was to resort to science fiction and fantasy literature. One of mine was to resort to sexual infidelity. It was a resort of which I am not proud. It was hurtful to Lily and hurtful to some other women. I would rather not have to mention it here.
>
> My sexual infidelity is a glaring example of the unreasonableness of romance. I would never have been diagnosed as a full-blown "sex addict," but in some ways it surely was a compulsion. A purely rational human being would know better. I, however, am not purely rational, and this irrational part of me had to

have its due. I might not have survived otherwise, but always wished I could have been a different kind of person who did not need such an outlet. And I always knew that my infidelities were potentially dangerous and destructive, not only to others but to myself. In a very real sense I was engaging in them despite myself (1995, pp. 28-30).

5. The *law of unintended consequences* teaches a purposeful action often has an unplanned result. Moviemakers have capitalized on this law in several productions involving unfaithfulness. In *Fatal Attraction* a man has an extramarital affair with a sociopathic woman who attempts to murder his wife (1987). The movie ends with the wife killing the woman in self-defense. In *Unfaithful* a married woman has a sexual liaison with a handsome womanizer (2002). The unforeseen consequence is the betrayed husband's murder of his wife's lover. Similarly, *Presumed Innocent* is the story of a betrayed wife who murders her husband's lover in order to preserve the marriage (1990). *Crimes and Misdemeanors* is a non-comedic Woody Allen movie in which an adulterous husband decides the only way to extricate himself from his affair is to have his mistress murdered (1989).

Unfortunately, real life also provides instances of infidelity with unintended consequences. The introduction to *It Happened in Little Valley* sets the stage for the true story of 12 minutes of tragedy that occurred in a small Western New York town in 1956:

The murder of Sue Ann Riggs by her husband, Ralph Riggs and subsequent suicide of her lover, Albert Roy Marsh, were the culmination of ordinary people engaged in ordinary circumstances. Ralph and Sue had a troubled marriage; Albert had recently divorced; Sue and Albert were having an affair. These circumstances hardly constitute a perfect storm for tragedy, but tragedy occurred in the early morning of November 28, 1956 in Little Valley, New York, the ordinary village in which they lived (Malikow, 2016, p. 1).

Another real-life instance of the *law of unintended consequences* manifesting as an extramarital affair occurred several years ago with a couple who engaged me for marital counseling. They had been involved in a *menage a trois*, an arrangement in which three people share a sexual relationship. The bisexual husband had convinced his wife it would be a delightful adventure if a man joined them in bed. The unanticipated problem was the extramarital affair that resulted. The wife fell in love with the invited man. In counseling the enraged husband said, "How could she do this to me? We promised each other there would be no sex that didn't involve the three of us" They eventually agreed to a trial separation which culminated in divorce.

Two Situations in Which Infidelity Might Not Be Morally Wrong

As previously stated, it's not challenging to defend monogamy in a marriage or faithfulness in a relationship. But making a case for non-exclusivity in a relationship is counterintuitive. Nevertheless, there are at least two situations in which a sexual tryst might not be immoral.

1. When both parties agree to an open relationship there is no disloyalty. One researcher, Dr. Lucille Ostertag, reported, "Some of the strongest unions I studied included spouses who each were involved in repeated extramarital affairs throughout the relationship. My findings have turned our preconceived notion of monogamy on its head" (Bett, 2002). While admitting not every extramarital affair is good, Ostertag observed, "It's inevitable (in marriages) for some familiarity to set in. But by bringing a little variety in, with new short-term partners, you can keep a relationship healthy and strong for many years to come" (2002).

Ostertag emphasized the necessity of maintaining four rules if an extramarital affair is enriching to a marriage: (1) no local engagements, the encounter must be distant from home; (2) agree to a "don't ask, don't tell" policy; (3) live guilt-free; and (4) "one-night stands" only, which means no subsequent contact with the paramour.

Dr. Ostertag is not the only social scientist to encounter the possibility of a benefit from infidelity. Sonya Friedman, a psychologist and author, conducted 100 interviews with women who claimed their extramarital affairs enabled them to remain in their marriages. Friedman does not advocate for infidelity in her book, *Secret Loves: Women with Two Lives*, but reports her subjects believe without an affair they could not have remained in their marriages (1994).

2. As unlikely as it seems, unfaithfulness might not be morally wrong when it's impossible for the betrayed party to know of the affair. Several years ago I encountered a man whose wife was in a PVS (persistent vegetative state) as a result of brain disease. Also referred to as "post coma unresponsiveness" (PCU), it is a state in which the cerebral cortex is not functioning, depriving the patient of the ability to perceive and think as well as produce and understand language. In this state there is no response to stimuli, merely the continuation of respiration, circulation, and a normal sleep cycle.

The husband admitted to me that he met with a woman once or twice a month to engage in sex. He enjoyed her company but did not love her and had no intention of abandoning his marriage. The woman understood and accepted the conditions of their relationship. "My wife is well-cared for," he told me, "I can afford excellent nursing care so she is able to live in our home. I love her. She'll never know about the other woman in my life."

Apart from individual accounts, I was unable to find a culture in which unfaithfulness is morally acceptable. Contrary to widespread belief, the Geisha tradition in Japan does not include sexual involvement. A Geisha is a woman trained to provide musical and dance entertainment in addition to serving a meal and engaging in conversation with a male guest.

XI. Can We Be Good Without God?

Why do you call me good? No one is good except God alone.
- Jesus (Luke 18:19)

The claim that people cannot be good without God does not mean the lives of all believers are morally superior to the lives of all unbelievers. Neither does it mean human beings are incapable of virtuous acts unless they are believers. Moreover, it does not mean believers will always demonstrate moral excellence. History compels the concessions that human decency is possible without God and professed believers have perpetrated evil. Concerning the former, the atheist and existentialist writer Albert Camus was a decent, compassionate man. Regarding the latter, the Reverend Jim Jones orchestrated the mass suicide of nearly an entire congregation, resulting in 913 deaths.

The assertion that people cannot be good without God is vulnerable to being misunderstood. "It would seem arrogant and ignorant to claim that those who do not share a belief in God do not often live good moral lives" (Craig, 2015). Anyone who opposes the assertion that people cannot be good without God by claiming it means all believers are morally superior to all unbelievers is committing the "straw man fallacy." (In argumentation the "straw man fallacy" occurs when an easily refuted position is assigned to an opponent, one the opponent neither stated nor would endorse, and that position is attacked and effortlessly defeated. The defeated position is the "straw man" because it is knocked over as easily as a scarecrow made of straw.)

Then what does it mean to say people cannot be good without God? It means if God does not exist then morality is merely a human convention. Without a moral authority that provides principles of conduct that are binding upon all human beings it is impossible to characterize any behavior as good or bad. An idea (not a precise quotation) found in Fyodor Dostoevsky's *The Brothers Karamazov* is: if there is no God, everything is permitted. Everything is permitted in the sense that there is no basis for declaring any behavior as bad. The goodness of people is not a question of our ability to perform a commendable act but how any act can be considered commendable if there is no standard for determining commendable acts. Recall from chapter I this is the question addressed by Jesus in his encounter with an unnamed wealthy man, narrated in Luke's gospel:

A certain ruler asked him, "Good teacher, what must I do to inherit eternal life?" "Why do you call me good?" Jesus answered. "No one is good – except God alone" (Luke 18:18,19).

The question, "Can people be good without God?" gives rise to a fundamental question: Is a discussion of good even a possibility without a meta-standard for human behavior? Philosopher Richard C. Taylor has written, "Contemporary writers in ethics, who blithely discourse on right and wrong and moral obligations without any reference to religion, are really just weaving intellectual webs from thin air, which amounts to saying they discourse without meaning" (1985, pp. 2-3). Taylor insists moral obligations cannot exist unless there is a being to whom they are owed:

> A duty is something that is owed. But something can be owed only to some person or persons. There can be no such thing as duty in isolation. But what if this higher-than-human lawgiver is no longer taken into account? Does the concept of moral obligation still make sense? The concept of moral obligation (is) unintelligible apart from the idea of God? (pp. 83-84).

Can definitive moral standards be derived from social conventions or nature? If not God, are there alternatives for a moral authority binding upon the human race? The humanist philosopher Paul Kurtz recognized the significance of this question when he wrote, "The central questions about ethical and moral principles concern (their) ontological foundation. If they are neither derived from God nor anchored in some transcendent ground, are they purely ephemeral?" (1988, p. 65). Kurtz advocated secular humanism, a philosophy that rejects religion as the source for morality and embraces reason and nature for determining ethics. He believed, "The moral principles that govern our behavior are rooted in habit and custom, feeling and fashion" (p. 73). However, yet another concession compelled by history is "habit and custom, feeling and fashion" greatly vary from culture to culture as well as within a culture over time. This is not to posit that all customs are moral expressions. A gentleman rising to stand when a lady enters the room is a matter of etiquette, not morality. The same is true of the erstwhile Japanese practice of a woman walking behind a man, however repugnant that convention might be to some contemporary Americans. In contrast, the practice of one human being owning another does have moral implications. The antisemitic attitude that resulted in millions of deaths in Nazi concentration camps cannot be dismissed as an amoral feeling. Professor Kurtz's observation that social conventions provide moral authority is a reiteration of moral relativism, which posits that morality is regionally determined. As such, his position shares relativism's problem of explaining why one culture's attitudes and practices should be preferred over another's.

The British philosopher Jamie Whyte is an unrestrained critic of relativism. Referring to relativism as a "morality fever" he writes,

> Cultural relativism is so absurd that it is hard to believe anyone can be so fevered as to assert it. If it were true, gods, planets, bacteria, and everything else would come into and go out of existence according to what people generally believe to exist which they obviously do not. A belief cannot be true in Iran but false in

Papua, New Guinea. If it is false anywhere it is false everywhere (2003, pp. 154-155).

Another suggested source for definitive moral standards is nature - the physical world with all its features and living things. Sociobiology, the field of science that attempts to explain social behavior in terms of evolution, theorizes that traits and behaviors that contribute to a specie's survival are genetically transmitted. The problem with this paradigm when it is applied to morality is instinctive behavior is not subject to moral evaluation. John Hick, a philosopher and theologian, distinguishes instinct from moral behavior with his hypothetical soldier ant: Suppose it (the ant) is called upon to immolate himself for the sake of the ant-hill.

> He feels the powerful pressure of instinct pushing himself towards self-destruction. But he asks himself why he should voluntarily carry out the suicidal programme to which instinct prompts him. Why should he regard the future existence of a million other ants as more important than his own continued existence? Since all that he is and has or ever can have is his own present existence, surely insofar as he is free from the domination of the blind force of instinct he will opt for life - his own life (1971, p. 63).

Further, if survival of the fittest is the rule of nature why should human beings have an obligation to any endangered species? No plant, insect, fish or animal is insisting on human assistance in its struggle for survival and reproduction. Moreover, if perpetuation of the human species is the goal from which moral authority is derived, what is special about human beings? Speaking to Rosencrantz, Shakespeare's Hamlet expresses his disdain for the claim that man is the pinnacle of creation:

> What a piece of work is a man! How noble in reason, how infinite in faculty! In form and moving how express and admirable! In action how like an angel, in apprehension how like a god! The beauty of the world. The paragon of animals. And yet, to me, what is this quintessence of dust? Man delights not me. No, nor woman neither though by your smiling you seem to say so (Act II, Scene 2).

Those who agree with Hamlet might be unimpressed with man owing to his penchant for self-destruction.

While evolutionists explain morality in terms of humanity's survival instinct, others point to what seems a determination to bring an end to human existence. Columnist and political commentator Charles Krauthammer has speculated we are alone in the universe in spite of astronomer Frank Drake's probabilistic argument to the contrary:

> Modern satellite data, applied to the Drake Equation, suggest the number (of extraterrestrial civilizations)

should be very high. So why the silence? Carl Sagan (among others) thought that the answer is to be found, tragically, in the high probability that advanced civilizations destroy themselves. In other words, this silent universe is not conveying a flattering lesson about our uniqueness but a tragic story about our destiny. It is telling us that intelligence may be the most cursed faculty in the entire universe - an endowment not just ultimately fatal but, on the scale of cosmic time, nearly instantly so (2013, p. 128).

Conclusion

All the preceding is not intended as an argument for the existence of God or a transcendent being. Rather, the purpose of what has been presented is to articulate and evaluate three possible sources for universal moral standards. Christian apologist William Lane Craig believes it is rational to envision moral chaos if a supreme being does not exist:

If God does not exist, then it is plausible to think that there are no objective moral values, that we have no moral duties, and that there is no moral accountability for how we live and act. The horror of such a morally neutral world is obvious (2015, p. 4).

Indeed, a morally neutral world would be horrific. However, even if it is true that only God could provide a definitive, indisputable code of conduct binding upon humanity, this would be insufficient to prove the existence of God. The argument that God must exist lest there be moral chaos is not a compelling argument, however appealing it might be to some. Something can be useful but not actually exist. (The mythical list that Santa Claus checks twice is useful for managing a child's behavior.) Friedrich Nietzsche believed the death of God and its collateral moral chaos was a favorable reality. He believed the absence of a universal lawgiver and judge would force people to construct their own moral codes and take responsibility for living or not living in accordance with them.

The aforementioned problems associated with cultural traditions and sociobiology as sources of moral authority rule them out as possibilities. This leaves a transcendent being as the most rational alternative. Certainly Craig believes this to be the case: "(If) we hold, as it seems rational to do, that objective moral values and duties do exist, then we have good grounds for believing in the existence of God" (p. 4).

In contrast to Craig, physician and author Robert Buckman concludes his book, *Can We Be Good Without God?* with these words:

> I am not particularly afraid of dying. I don't necessarily look forward to it. But in my own case, my feelings about my own death and dying are not enough to make me consider a belief in a supernatural God as an option (2002, p. 259).

Epilogue: Chaos in a Parking Lot

The implications of moral chaos can be discerned from the following mundane incident. Smith parks his car in a "Handicap Parking Only" parking place at the supermarket. Jones, not handicapped, correctly notes Smith's car does not have a handicap parking permit in the windshield or a handicap driver license plate. Further, Jones watches an obviously healthy young man emerge from his car.

Smith's female companion says to him, "You're breaking the law. You've parked in a handicap only spot."

Laughing, Smith replies, "Honey, there are no rules in a parking lot."

Hearing this, Jones parks his car behind Smith's, pinning Smith's car is between a light post and Jones' car. An hour later Jones, finished with his shopping, returns to his car. An irate Smith confronts him, shrieking, "What the (expletive) is wrong with you, parking like this? Are you crazy or a (expletive) idiot?"

Not the least intimidated, Jones responds, "Honey, there are no rules in a parking lot."

XII. Is a Moral Life a Good Life and Is a Good Life a Moral Life?

The good life is active, contemplative, somewhat fatalistic, and selfless.

- Daniel Robinson

Epicurus taught, "It is impossible to live the pleasant life without living sensibly, nobly and justly, and it is impossible to live sensibly, nobly and justly without living pleasantly" (2015). What did Epicurus have in mind when he spoke of a pleasant life? It is unlikely he meant a life of pleasure and ease. Many a person has lived a painful, depressed life in spite of having lived "sensibly, nobly and justly." No one lived a more virtuous life than Jesus Christ, yet he was "a man of sorrows, and familiar with suffering" (Isaiah 53:3). Moreover, the psalmist in the Hebrew Bible was troubled by the pleasant life of the wicked:

> My feet had almost slipped; I had nearly lost my foothold. For I envied the arrogant when I saw the prosperity of the wicked. They have no struggles; their bodies are healthy and strong. They are free from the burdens common to man; they are not plagued by human ills (Psalm 73: 2-5).

The prophet Jeremiah made an equally hyperbolic statement in the form of a question when he asked God:

> Why does the way of the wicked prosper? Why do all the faithless live at ease? You have planted them and they have taken root; they grow and bear fruit. You are always on their lips but far from their hearts (Jeremiah 12:1-2).

The distinguished professor Peter Kreeft, when asked if virtue always brings happiness, responded, "It seems that it obviously does not, for we see that virtuous people are often dour, while the wicked laugh." (2012, p. 167).

For Epicurus a pleasant life is not necessarily a happy life. Rather, a pleasant life is a life that is pleasing to the one living it, and this requires a life that is consistent with that individual's moral code. Aristotle also believed this and taught a virtuous life is necessary for *eudaimonia* (the flourishing life). In the *Nicomachean Ethics* he offers this assessment: "He is happy who lives in accordance with complete virtue and is sufficiently equipped with external goods, not for some chance period but throughout a complete life" (2009, 1101a10). A failure to live consistently with one's own moral code is exemplified by Reverend Dimmesdale, the character in Nathaniel Hawthorne's novel, *The Scarlet Letter* referred to in chapter II.

In addition, Aristotle believed an upright life is the intended life for human beings. Just as the *telos* (purpose) of a knife is to cut, the purpose of a human being is to live a virtuous life. *The Life We Prize*, a little known but brilliant treatise by the Quaker theologian David Elton Trueblood, includes an arresting observation concerning life and death:

> Each of us is bound to die, and every rational person is highly conscious that his life is short, but there need be no tragedy in this. It is surely not so bad to die, providing one has really lived before he dies. Life need not be long to be good, for indeed it cannot be long. The tragedy is not that all die, but that so many fail to really live (1951, p. 164).

Of course, Trueblood's assertion raises the question: If longevity is not necessary for a good life then what constitutes a good life? Both classical antiquity and the Christian tradition encourage a life lived in accord with the *four cardinal virtues*: temperance (self-discipline), fortitude (courage), justice (fairness), and prudence (wisdom). A composite of a good life derived from various philosophical and literary works characterize a good life as one that is lived fully, honorably, meaningfully, existentially, regretlessly, and redemptively. Each of these six characteristics is described in the following subsections.

Live Fully

In his poem, "To the Virgins, to make much of Time," Robert Herrick writes:

Gather ye rosebuds while ye may,
Old time is still a-flying:
And this young flower that smiles today
Tomorrow will be dying (1648, number 208).

In the movie *Dead Poets Society* Mr. Keating, an English teacher played by Robin Williams, instructs his students that Herrick is imploring the reader to *carpe diem*, translated from Latin to English as, "seize the day" (1989). Edgar Guest expresses a similar idea in his poem, "Results and Roses:"

It matters not what goal you seek
Its secret here reposes:
You've got to dig from week to week
To get results or roses (1950, p. 23)

Live Honorably

Speaking at the 1992 Boston University Commencement, Fred "Mister" Rogers encouraged the graduates to, "Live in such a way that you'll never be ashamed of the truth about yourself" (05/17/92). Shakespeare also expresses the value of a good reputation in *Othello*:

Good name in man and woman, dear my lord,
Is the immediate jewel of their souls.

Who steals my purse steals trash; 'tis something,
nothing;
But he that filches from me my good name
Robs me of that which not enriches him,
And makes me poorer indeed (Act III, Scene 3)

Live Meaningfully

When asked the age-old question, "What is the meaning of life?" Sigmund Freud expressed agreement with Leo Tolstoy when he responded, "love and work" (2015). In contrast, Viktor Frankl wrote the meaning of life cannot be reduced to a few words or principles: "In an age in which the Ten Commandments seem to many people to have lost their unconditional validity, man must learn to listen to the ten thousand commandments of which his life consists" (1969, p. x). He believed the meaning of life changes from situation to situation and in each circumstance each of us bears responsibility for making that situation personally meaningful.

Live Existentially

Existentialism is a philosophical movement associated with Soren Kierkegaard and Friedrich Nietzsche in the nineteenth century and Martin Heidegger, Jean-Paul Sartre, and Albert Camus in the twentieth century. The hallmarks of existentialism are freedom and responsibility. Sartre writes, "... man is condemned to be free. Condemned, because he did not create himself, yet, in other respects free; because, once thrown into the world, he is responsible for everything he does" (1957, p. 23). Closely related to living meaningfully, living existentially means we bear responsibility for the consequences of our actions. Awareness of this accountability provides moral guidance.

Live Regretlessly

Hockey legend Wayne Gretsky said, "You miss one-hundred percent of the shots you don't take" (2015). And John Greenleaf Whittier writes,

"For of all sad words of tongue or pen.
The saddest are these: "It might have been!"
(1856, 106-107).

Psychologist Erik Erikson proposed the *Psychosocial Theory of Human Development*, positing we pass through eight stages from cradle to grave. The final developmental task, "integrity vs. despair," is retrospection. It is the stage at which we reflect on our lives and accomplishments. If we're content with how we've lived, we face death with a sense of satisfaction (integrity). If, on the other hand, we are disappointed by misappropriated time and unachieved goals we approach death with regret (despair).

Live Redemptively

The verb redeem means to take that which is unpleasant or distressing and make it useful or, at least, tolerable. Redemptive is the adjective form of redeem and redemption is its noun form. It's not an overstatement to say no one has written about a redemptive life with more clarity and meaning than Viktor Frankl. The epilogue of his classic, *Man's Search for Meaning*, is entitled "Tragic Optimism." There he enumerates life's three unavoidable tragedies: pain, guilt, and death. He believed everyone has the ability to redeem these inevitable calamities. Pain can be redeemed by using it to become more compassionate. The poet Betty Sue Flowers captures this idea with these words: "Pain is a mechanism for growth; it carves out the heart and allows room for compassion" (Cronkite, 1995, p. 315). Guilt is redeemable if it leads to repentance and a commitment to change. As for death, Frankl believed life's transitoriness provides "an incentive to take responsible action'" (1959, p. 162).

Ronald Cotton knows what it means to live redemptively. Wrongfully convicted of rape in 1985 and sentenced to life imprisonment, he served ten years in a North Carolina prison before DNA evidence exonerated him. Not only has he forgiven the woman who erroneously identified him, he has co-authored a book with her (2009). In addition, he has spoken at numerous conferences and law schools on the fallibility of eye witnesses.

Closing Thought

Concerning the relationship between virtue and happiness Kreeft writes,

> "Virtue is its own reward." Doing good for the sake of doing good is true morality, whereas doing good in order to attain happiness is self-serving and mercenary and not truly moral. "A good conscience is your best pillow"; but moral virtue should not be pursued simply as a sleeping pill, or as the means to the end of personal happiness, for that is egotism.
>
> Happiness (blessedness) is virtue's *natural* fruit; it is to virtue what marriage is to courtship, victory to battle, or muscle strength to exercise. The reward for a life of virtue is not external and mercenary but the natural and inevitable consummation of that life itself: that happiness cannot be separated from virtue (2012, pp. 167, 169).

References

Introduction

Korn, M. (2013). "Does an 'A' in Ethics Have Any Value?" The Wall Street Journal. February 6, 2013.

Schaub, M. (2012). "Can you teach ethics?" Mays Business School. College Station, TX: Texas A & M University. November 26, 2012.

Velasquez, M., Andre, C., Shanks, T., and Meyer, M. (1987). "Can ethics be taught?" Santa Clara University. Santa Clara, CA: Markkula Center for Applied Ethics. January 1, 1987.

Chapter I

A dangerous method. (2011). London, UK: Lionsgate.

Heinlein, R. (2005). *Of the main sequence.* New York: Doubleday: Science Fiction Book Club.

Hemingway, E. (1932). *Death in the afternoon.* New York: Charles Scribner's Sons.

Kilpatrick, W. (1992). *Why Johnny can't tell right from wrong: Moral illiteracy and the case for character education.* New York: Simon & Schuster.

King, M.L. (1997). *Letters of a nation.* Andrew Carroll (Editor). New York: Random House. Broadway Books.

_____ (1967). Speech given to The Hungry Club in Atlanta, GA on May 10, 1967.

Malikow, M. (2007). *Heroism as virtue: Reflecting on human greatness.* Chipley, FL: Theocentric Publishing.

Orwell, G. (1946). *Why I write.* New York: Penguin Group.

Seligman, M. and Peterson, C. (2004). *Character strengths and virtues.* Oxford, UK: Oxford University Press.

Chapter II

Aristotle. (2009). *Nichomachean ethics.* Lesley Brown (Editor). David Rose (Translator). Oxford, UK: Oxford University Press.

Bausman, C. (2016). "Leave no man behind: Implications, criticisms, and rationale." mtntactical.com> knowledge>leave-no-man-behind. September 2, 2016.

Bethge, E. (200). *Dietrich Bonhoeffer: A biography.* Minneapolis, MN: Fortress Press.

Epicurus. (2015). "Letter to Menoeceus." Recovered from www.epicurus.net website April 2015.

Edwards, J. (1992). "Sinners in the hands of an angry God." Pensacola, FL: Christian Life Books.

Hawthorne, N. (1978). *The scarlet letter.* New York: Norton.

Jacoby, J. (2013). "Where does compassion come from?" *New York Times.* September 15, 2013.

Kant, I. (1785). *Grounding for the metaphysics of morals: On a supposed right to lie because of philanthropic concerns.* J.W. Ellington, translator. 1993. Indianapolis, IN: Hackett Classics.

Les Miserables (1980). Premiere September 24, 1980 in Paris, France.

Myers, D. (1992). The pursuit of happiness: Who is happy and why. New York: William Morrow and   Company.

Chapter III

Aristotle. (2014). Recovered from Thinkexist.com website October, 2014.

Durkheim, E. (1897). Le suicide: etudie de sociologie. Paris, France: Alcan.

Grisham, J. (1989). *A time to kill*. Chatham, NJ: Wynwood Press Publishing.

Hare, R. (1999). *Without conscience: The disturbing world of the psychopaths among us*. New York: Guilford Press.

Harris, S. (2020). *Making sense: Conversations on consciousness, morality, and the future of humanity*. New York: HarperCollins Publishers.

Holmbach, P. (1770). "The illusion of free will. Reason and responsibility." Readings in some basic problems in philosophy. Belmont, CA: Wadsworth/Thompson Learning.

James, W. (1891). "The moral philosopher and the moral life." Address to the Yale Philosophical Club, published in the *International Journal of Ethics*, April, 1891.

Jamison, K.R. (1995). *An unquiet mind*. New York: Random House.

Joiner, T. (2011). *Myths about suicide*. Cambridge, MA: Harvard University Press.

Katen, T. (1973). *Doing philosophy*. Englewood Cliffs, NJ: Prentice-Hall.

Kuklinski, R. (2003). "The ice man interviews: The psychiatrist and the ice man." New York: HBO Videos.

Malikow, M. (2009). *Philosophy 101: A primer for the apathetic or struggling student*. Lanham, MD: University Press of America.

_____. (2013). *The human predicament: Towards an understanding of the human condition*. Chipley, FL: Theocentric Publishing Group.

Milgram, S. (1963). "Behavior study of obedience." *Journal of Abnormal & Social Psychology*, 67(4). 371-378.

Morton, A. (2004). *On evil: Thinking in action*. New York: Routledge.

Negri, P. (1999). *The wit and wisdom of Mark Twain*. Mineola, NY: Dover Publications.

Nuland, S. (1993). *How we die. Reflections on life's final chapter*. New York: Random House.

Tennyson, A. (1854). "The charge of the light brigade." Recovered from The Poetry Foundation website. Harriet Monroe Poetry Institute. Chicago, IL. October 2014.

Thayer, J. (1996). *Thayer's Greek – English lexicon of the new testament*. Peabody, MA: Hendrickson Publishers.

Wallace, D.F. (2007). *Consider the lobster and other essays*. New York: Little, Brown and Company.

Chapter IV

Benatar, D. (2012). *Better never to have been: The harm of coming into existence*. Oxford, UK: Oxford University Press.

Bentham, J. (2014). Recovered from Thinkexist.com website November 2014.60

Coles, J. (1995). *The story of Ruby Bridges*. New York: Scholastic Paperbacks

_____. (1998). *The moral intelligence of children: How to raise a moral child*. New York: Penguin Group.

deBeauvoir, S. (1954). *The ethics of ambiguity*. Seacaucus, NJ: Citadel Press.

Fletcher, J. (1966). *Situational ethics: The new morality*. Santa Ana, CA: Westminster Press.

_____. (2014). Recovered from Thinkexist.com website November 2014.

Haidt, J. (2006). *The happiness hypothesis: Finding modern truth in ancient wisdom*. New York: Perseus Books.

_____ (2012). *The righteous mind: Why good people are divided by politics and religion*. New York: Pantheon Books.

Harris, S. (2020). *Making sense: Conversations on consciousness, morality, and the future of humanity*. New York: HarperCollins Publishers.

Hill, G. (1987). *The discovery Bible: New American standard version*. Chicago. IL: Moody Press.

Hume, D. (1740). *A treatise of human nature*. Reprinted in 21012. Charleston, SC: CreateSpace Independent Publishing Platform.

Kant, I. (2014). Recovered from Thinkexist.com website November 2014.

_____. (1785). *Grounding for the metaphysics of morals: On a supposed right to lie because of philanthropic concerns.* J.W. Ellington, translator. 1993. Indianapolis, IN: Hackett Classics.

Malikow, M. (2014). *Mere existentialism: A primer.* Chipley, FL: Theocentric Publishing.

Milgram, S. (1974). *Obedience to authority: An experimental view.* New York: HarperCollins.

Mill, J.S. (2014). Recovered from Thinkexist.com website November 2014.

Nietzsche, F. (1974). *The gay science.* Walter Kaufmann, translator. New York: Random House.

_____. (1966). *Beyond good and evil.* Walter Kaufmann, translator. New York: Vintage Books.

Pascal, B. (2014). Recovered from Thinkexist.com website November 2014.

Peck M.S. (1983). *People of the lie: The hope for healing human evil.* New York: Simon and Schuster.

Sartre, J.P. (1957). *Existentialism and human emotions*. New York: Citadel Press. Kensington Publishing Corporation.

Truman, H.S. (1945). Statement by the President of the United States on August 6, 1945. Harry S. Truman Library. Independence, MO.

Chapter V.

Burke, E. (2015). *Philosophical enquiry into the origin of our ideas of the sublime and beautiful.* Oxford, UK: Oxford University Press.

Calley, W. (2015). "The trial of William Calley." Recovered from *Wikipedia*, January 2015.

Durant, W. (1926). *The story of philosophy: The lives and opinions of the world's greatest philosophers.* NY: Pocket Books.

Hare, R. (1999). *Without conscience: The disturbing world of psychopaths among us.* New York: Guilford Publications, Inc.

Harris, S. (2013). *Lying.* Carlsbad, CA: Four Elephants Press.

_____. (2020). *Making sense: Conversations on consciousness, morality, and the future of humanity.* New York: HarperCollins Publishers.

Hauser, T. (1991). *Muhammed Ali: His life and times.* New York: Simon and Schuster.

Heinlein, R. (2005). *Of the main sequence.* New York: Doubleday: Science Fiction Book Club.

Lewis, D. (1998). *Guilty by reason of insanity.* New York: Ivy Books.

Mann, L. (1981). "The baiting crowd in episodes o suicide." *Journal of Personality and Social Psychology.* 41(4): 703-709.

Martin, E. (2016). "14 reasons why good people do bad things." *Business Insider.* December 15, 2016.

Poe, E. (2016). *The black cat.* American Roots; Reprint Edition.

Seger, B. (1980). "Against the wind." Capitol Records.

Whitman, C. (1966). Recovered from toyiabr.wordpress.com/2017/08/26.charles-whitman's-suicide note/ on January 12, 2021.

Chapter VI

Gay, P. (1989). Freud: A life for our times. New York: W.W. Norton Company.

Kyle, C. (2015). Recovered from Brainy Quote website on April 27, 2015.

Oliner, S. (2003). *Do unto others: Extraordinary acts of ordinary people*. Boulder, CO: Westview Press.

Park, M., Grinberg, E., and Ap, T. (2016). "'We'd make the same decision' zoo director says of gorilla shooting." CNN US. May 31, 2016.

Chapter VII

Chua, A. (2011). *Battle hymn of the tiger mother*. New York: Penguin Group.

Harris, S. (2020). *Making sense: Conversations on consciousness, morality, and the future of humanity*. New York: HarperCollins Publishers.

Holdsworth, W.S. (1926). History of English law. London: Methuen.

Mintz, S. (2018). "Ethics Sage" blog. April 3, 2018.

Max Malikow

Chapter VIII

Boatright, J. (1993). *Ethics and the conduct of business*. New York: Prentice-Hall, Inc.

Farrar, E. (1997). *Letters of a nation*. Carroll, A. (editor). New York. Broadway Books.

Grenoble, R. (2013). "Ali Al-Khawajir, Saudi man sentenced to be paralyzed in 'eye for eye justice." *The Huffington Post*. April 4, 2013.

Harr, J. (1996). *A civil action*. New York: Vintage Press. Random House.

Huffington Post (2013). "Melissa Nelson, dental assistant, fired for being too attractive, disputes court ruling that sided with boss." January 10, 2013.

_____. (2012). "Father thirty times over seeks break in child support." Reported in *The Los Angeles Times* on May 18, 2012.

King, M.L. (1997). *Letters of a nation*. Andrew Carroll (Editor). New York: Random House. Broadway Books.

_____. (2001). *The autobiography of Martin Luther King, Jr*. New York: Warner Books, Inc.

Kinsella, W.B. (1982). *Shoeless Joe*. New York: Houghton Mifflin.

McVicker. (2000)."Billie Bob's misfortune." *The Houston Press*. February 10, 2000.

National Center for Education Statistics (2020). Recovered from www.businessinsider.com on January 28, 2021.

Rawls, J. (1971). *A theory of justice*. Cambridge, MA: Harvard University Press.

Sartre, J. (1957). *Existentialism and human emotions*. New York: Kensington Publishing Corporation.

Stossel, J. (1998). "The mystery of happiness: Who has it and how to get it." ABC News Special. Airing date: January 22, 1998.

Sullivan, P. "William 'Bud' Post III: Unhappy lottery winner. The Washington Post. January 20, 2013.

The Post Standard (2012). "Who decides what makes up a fair share?" Malikow, M. November 18, 2011.

Thoreau, H.D. (2014). *Civil disobedience*. Edinburgh, Scotland. Black and White Publishing.

Chapter IX.

American Heritage Dictionary. (1973). New York: American Heritage Publishing Company.

Bok, S. (1978). *Lying: Moral choice in public and private life*. New York: Random House.

Deveney, K. "Liar, Liar, Parents on Fire." *Newsweek*. 04/07/2008.

Frankl, V. (1959). *Man's search for meaning*. New York: Washington Square Books.

Fridman, S. (1994). *Secret loves: Women with two loves*. New York: Crown Publishing.

Kohlberg, L. (1984). *The psychology of moral development: Essays on moral development* (Vol. 2). San Francisco: Harper and Row.

MacLaskey and MacLaskey. (1920). Clarence Darrow - Frederick Starr Debate: "Is Life Worth Living?" Garrick Theatre. Chicago, IL: 03/28/20.

Martin, M. (1986). *Everyday morality: An introduction to applied ethics.* Belmont, CA: Wadsworth Publishing Company.

_____. 1995). Everyday morality: An introduction to applied ethics. Belmont, CA: Wadsworth Publishing Company.

Milgram, S. (2005). *Obedience to authority.* New York: Pinter and Martin.

Rand, A. (1961). *The virtue of selfishness.* New York: Penguin Books.

Rosenhan, D. (1973). "On being sane in insane places." *Science, 179*, 250-258.

Seligman, M. and Peterson, C. (2004). *Character strengths and virtues: A handbook and classification.* New York: Oxford University Press.

Chapter X

Bett, M. (2002). "New study reveals cheating makes your marriage stronger." Recovered from http://sprott. physics.wisc.edu/pickover/pc/marriage_cheat.html on March 1, 2013.

Crimes and Misdemeanors. (1989). Orion Pictures.

Fatal Attraction. (1987). Paramount Pictures.

Huffington Post. (2013). "What is cheating? A new study looks at different definitions of infidelity." Posted on 02/01/2013.

Malikow, M. (2016). *It happened in Little Valley: A case study of uxoricide.* Chipley, FL: Theocentric Publishing.

Moore, T. (1999). *The soul of sex.* New York: Harper Perennial.

Peck, M.S. (1995). *In search of stones.* New York: Hyperion Books.

Presumed Innocent. (1990). Warner Brothers.

Unfaithful (2002). Twentieth Century Fox.

Viorst, J. 1998. *Necessary losses: The loves, illusions, dependencies and impossible expectations that all of us have to give up in order to grow.* New York. Simon and Schuster.

Waller, R. (1992). *The bridges of Madison county.* New York: Warner Books, Inc.

Chapter XI

Buckman, R. (2002). *Can we be good without God? Biology, behavior, and the need to believe.* Amherst, NY: Prometheus Books.

Craig, W.L. (2015). *Can we be good without God?* Recovered from Reasonable Faith website on 03/18/2015.

Hick, J. (1971). *Arguments for the existence of God.* New York: Herder and Herder.

Krauthammer, C. (2013). *Things that matter: Three decades of passions, pastimes, and politics.* New York: Crown Forum.

Kurtz, P. (1988). *Forbidden fruit.* Buffalo, NY: Prometheus Books.

Taylor, R.C. (1984). Ethics, faith, and reason. Englewood Cliffs, NJ: Prentice-Hall.

Whyte, J. (2004). *Crimes against logic: Exposing the bogus arguments of politicians, priests, journalists, and other serial offenders.* New York: McGraw – Hill.

Chapter XII

Aristotle. (2009). *Nichomachean ethics*. Lesley Brown (editor). David Rose (translator). Oxford, UK: Oxford University Press.

Cronkite, C. (1995). *On the edge of darkness: Conversations about conquering depression*. New York: Doubleday.

Dead Poets Society. (1989). Burbank, CA: Touchstone Pictures.

Epicurus. (2015). "Letter to Menoeceus." Recovered from www.epicurus.net website April 2015.

Frankl, V. (1969). *The will to meaning: Foundations and applications of logotherapy*. New York: Penguin Group.

_____. (1959). *Man's search for meaning*. New York: Washington Square.

Freud, S. (2015). Recovered from Thinkexist.com website March, 2015.

Gretsky, W. (2015). Recovered from Thinkexist.com website March 2015.

Guest, E. (1950). "Results and roses." Recovered from All Poetry.com website April 2015.

Herrick, R. (1648). "To the virgins to make much of time." Recovered from All Poetry.com website April 2015.

Kreeft. (2012). *Summa philosophica*. South Bend, IN: St. Augustine's Press.

Sartre, J.P. (1957). *Existentialism and human emotions*. New York: Kensington Publishing Group.

Trueblood. D.E. (1951). *The life we prize*. New York: Harper and Brothers.

Whittier, J.G. (1856). "Maude Miller." Recovered from www.poetry.com April 2015.

About the Author

Max Malikow brings 35 years of teaching philosophy to addressing the question, "Why be good?" He earned a Bachelor's degree from the University of Nebraska, Master's degree from Gordon-Conwell Theological Seminary, and doctorate from Boston University. He is on the faculty of the Renee Crown Honors Program of Syracuse University and an Adjunct Assistant Professor of Philosophy at LeMoyne College. The author or editor of 18 previous books, he is a practicing psychotherapist in Syracuse, New York.

Other Books by Max Malikow

Why is Life So Difficult? Reflections and Suggestions.

Six Paths to a Good Life

Heroism and Virtue: Reflections on Human Greatness

Buried Above Ground: Understanding Suicide and the Suicidal Mind

Christ the Counselor: Reflecting on Jesus as a Therapist.

It Happened in Little Valley: A Case Study of Uxoricide

Death: Reflections on the End of Life and What Comes After.

Mere Existentialism: A Primer

It's Not Too Late! Making the Most of the Rest of Your Life (third edition)

The Human Predicament: Towards an Understanding of the Human Situation

Philosophy Reader: Essays and Articles for Thought and Discussion

Being Human: Philosophical Reflections on Psychological Issues

Philosophy 101: A Primer for the Apathetic or Struggling Student

Suicidal Thoughts: Essays on Self-Determined Death

Profiles in Character: Twenty-Six Stories that Will Instruct and Inspire Teenagers

Teachers for Life: Advice and Methods Gathered Along the Way

What Is Philosophy and Why Study It? The Case for Relevance

Living When a Young Friend Commits Suicide: Or Is Even Thinking About It (co-authored with Rabbi Dr. Earl A. Grollman)